CEREAL DATING

Cereal Dating
Love, Lies and Leftovers After Fifty
Audie A. Mae

ISBN: 978-1-967628-04-9 | Pub Date: October 14, 2025
Paperback | $18.95

Emerald Books
Bend, OR

 Emerald Books

Cereal Dating

Love, Lies & Leftovers After Fifty

by Audie A. Mae

Mom, you're my everything. I am nothing without you.
My brother and sister, you're the wind
beneath my wings—always.
My kids, it is my greatest privilege
and honor to be your mom.
AZ BFF, I'm so grateful for your editing,
encouragement, and support.

1. Cereal, anyone?

I always did love cereal. Not the sickening sweet kind and not the bland kind either. I often mix my cereals so that I have a perfect combination of flavors. My all-time favorite is a cranberry-almond crunch swimming in cold whole milk. Sometimes even with luscious cream if I am being especially reckless.

In my lifelong quest to find the perfect cereal, I have tried a wide variety. Raisin Bran, crunchy and sweet. Corn Pops previously known as Sugar Pops because we can't have sugar in the name for goodness sake, although the recipe is still chock-full of sugar. Sugar Pops, Corn Pops, . . . , no matter what they're called, I still love them. The newer, healthy high-protein varieties are enticing, in moderation of course. Cereal can be the perfect nightcap, even though most people prefer to eat it in the morning.

Choosing a cereal and when to consume it is ironically like choosing a man. I never met a cereal that I didn't like; however, there are some kinds that I prefer way more than others. Everyone likes different brands. The timing is subject to individual preference as well. I most often eat cereal at night, but I'd say the majority of people eat in the morning.

I am probably what most would consider to be a cereal dater. I embrace it, just as I have with trying cereals all these years. If variety is the spice of life, why not apply that principle to dating? Why not try dating people who you think you may not like. You could be surprised. Cereal that you loved as a kid may repulse you now. The same holds true for dating. You may realize that you *do* love the snap, crackle, and pop of Rice Krispies after all. Being a cereal dater is just another way of saying you are trying a variety of types until you decide which one you like the most. My stepbrother met his second wife on a dating app. His now wife had a free trial on Bumble that was about to expire. They had been messaging on the app, but she was running out of time, so she says she took a huge chance and decided to give him her email address. She had heard horror stories and was worried about giving out her phone number. I assumed that like most of us she had been out with several guys before she met him. But, no! He was the one and only guy she dated. The only guy! They have been married ten years now. She didn't need to try all the cereals; she chose one and lived happily ever after.

To each their own. I prefer trying them all. I highly recommend checking out the world of on-line dating because dating can be fun. For me dating provided a much-needed escape for my trying life situation. I have loved meeting men from all walks of life, hearing their stories, laughing, and just getting out of my bubble. I hugged and/ or kissed each one upon meeting them because I was very happy to be there, no matter the outcome.

2. Over the Hill

Is fifty the new forty? It must be because I feel so much younger than my parents were at this age. Maybe because my kids are young? When my dad turned forty, his friends gave him a gag gift. It was a large square "skateboard" with four little wheels in the corners. He promptly stood on his new skateboard for the elderly for thirty seconds, then fell and broke his arm. At the time, he seemed to be about ninety. My mom, who acted and looked much younger, became a widow in her forties. (Don't worry . . . it wasn't the skateboard that ended it for Dad).

After Dad passed, Mom dated up a storm, meeting people at the golf course, on trips, at nightclubs . . . She serendipitously reunited with a former Little League coach at a funeral. I happened to be with her and his parting words were, "Goodbye, beautiful ladies, one for the father and one for the son." He had four handsome sons. At the time, I was dating someone, so I never considered the option, but I laughed at the sentiment. I asked her on the car ride home if she would really be up for dating a man who was short and bald?! She giggled wisely and said, "Of course I would.."

Boy, did she choose wisely because what that bald guy lacked in height, he made up for in confidence, integrity, spirit, kindness and commitment. Naturally, they fell madly in love. He had no intention of getting married but alas divine intervention stepped in and sent him some signs from above. A rose bush bloomed that had never bloomed since his first wife had passed. So, after five years together they got engaged in their favorite chapel and then married a few months later. PopPop, as we lovingly call him, was quite the character. Nothing was typical about him. He didn't cuss, he didn't drink, he used to hop up in the air when he danced, and his voice would squeak when he was making a point. He brought stability, faith, and love to my mom. PopPop gave her the marriage she had always dreamed of. We were so lucky to have him in our lives. He was the best role model that the combined twelve grandkids could have ever had. We also gained four brothers who we love as well. She may have had a happy ending, but I am not sure about me. I don't have to tell you that things have changed since our parents were in their forties and fifties. If they were single, they had very limited dating opportunities while we have a world of opportunity via online dating. Or do we?

3. To cheat, or not to cheat?

Was that the question? Is that ever the question when you first get married? I think not. In fact, I think the majority of all the "marrieds" think they will never want to cheat. They have no idea what is in store for them, otherwise nobody would get married. Sooner or later, everyone has an opportunity to cheat. Eventually people consider, or it crosses their mind. Lots of people are unfaithful in a variety of ways. Some cheaters are very happily married, while others aren't. The desire to cheat often has nothing to do with your spouse. Sure, you can blame it on them, but it starts and ends with you. Your moral compass, core values, self-esteem and strength determine whether you will cheat. I think most "marrieds" consider the possibility at some point in their long and winding marriage journey. Cheating is the reason that most people get divorced. As my favorite DJ, Elliot on DC101, explains, "People divorce because they want to have sex with someone else."

I was married for nearly eighteen years to a conservative family man who professed his disdain for cheaters. He basically screamed from the rooftops that he would never cheat or leave me for any reason. Yes, his emphatic pronouncements against cheating should have been my first clue. I know that now. He claimed that he would stay with me forever unless . . . I cheated on him. Which is ironic. I was 100% faithful to him. Once after joining Facebook in my forties, a former college frat boy contacted me. He was the John Belushi of my college campus. An endearing, lovable man. He immediately revealed that he was divorced and had lost 100 pounds. He assumed the reason that we never hooked up was because he was, as he put it, the fat guy.

Frat Boy told me that I was one of two items on his bucket list. The other was for the CAPS to win the Stanley Cups and thankfully that happened in 2018. I've never heard anything more flattering prior to that or since then. At the time, I had been married for fourteen years with four kids, so it hit differently than it would have in my blissfully single thirties. Even though he buttered me up, I did not even consider seeing him. I did not engage with him or reveal any details about my marriage. It seems that oftentimes complaining about spouses is the entry into an affair. People act like affairs just happen out of the blue, but it usually starts with spouse bashing. Knowing that, and having no intention of cheating, my responses were always purely platonic.

My ex saw one of his crass texts where he said something about wanting me. At that point, I had to block him. I never saw him. Truth be told, I was proud of my marriage. I thought it was a partnership to be envied. I truly adored my spouse. In hindsight I wish I had cheated, something I have said often since my ex left. I guess I feel like it would not have changed the outcome if I did, and it would have been fun. Frat boy called me "kitten," and I doubt that anyone will call me that again. Maybe having sex with me would have been a major disappointment. In any case, I didn't cheat, and I wish I would have. Frat boy passed away after my divorce and we never had that bucket list reunion. I had other opportunities to cheat, like everyone else. Granted, being a stay-at-home mom, most of my opportunities consisted of men coming into my home for repairs, inspections, pest prevention, pool and pond maintenance. There were some mighty fine looking contractors, electricians, pool boys and the like. Then, of course, there were former colleagues and past loves, and plenty of those to choose from. I didn't cheat. Not. Once. I could have, but I didn't. My core values wouldn't allow for it. I was faithful to myself, my marriage, and my family. In retrospect though, where did that get me in the end? Divorced. It's a debate for another day.

4. How did I get here?

This is a place that I never, ever expected to be, but life has a crazy way of twisting and turning in an unpredictable manner. I will spare you the details of my painful and unexpected divorce that culminated after a house fire and ended in my spouse abandoning his four children to run away with another woman who he had vehemently denied having an affair with. My educated, high-level executive devoted husband left me and his kids, who were in seventh to ninth grade. Suddenly, I was thrown into the world of parenting teens alone. I was in shock and grieving the loss of my marriage. My life was in shambles, my kids no longer had a dad. So, after five months straight of crying my eyes out, I did what anyone would do in a firestorm of hell: I entered the uncharted world of online dating. Some friends thought it was too soon. Some felt like I was still married because the divorce wasn't final. I assured them that my attorney gave me the green light. I thought, *Well there's no time like the present! Everyone must do what works for them, on the advice of legal counsel.*

Keep in mind that dating doesn't exactly get easier or better with the passing of time. If I were thirty and childless, I might take the time to travel Europe, meditate, and "find myself" by hooking up with exotic foreigners, but I did not have that luxury. A single, gorgeous, and successful friend said, "What are you waiting for? Get out there, NOW!" So, I did. It has been quite a ride—an enjoyable ride, I must say.

Note: I DON'T recommend dating while you have several teenagers 24/7. It does "cramp your style," to put it mildly. Simply put, it's nearly impossible. I am not one to run from challenges and I wasn't getting any younger or better looking, as one of my bosses once said, so, with that in mind, I jumped in.

A Southern belle, life of the party friend, told me to keep track of the guys I date by making a list. She advised that it takes at least twenty-five dates to find one that you really connect with and have a potential relationship with. Basically, it is a numbers game. I thought to myself, nah, it will only take me ten tops. Now, ninety plus guys and counting later, I have become a cereal dater.

5. Dating back in the day

Where did you meet your spouse? College, work, high school? In the olden days, you met someone, dated them, fell in love, got engaged, then got married. Most were on a straight-and-narrow path to the altar and an illusive happily ever after. Some took more indirect paths. Patty met her future husband in the seventies, when she was eight. She lost her cat during a snowstorm. One of those nor'easters that produce mounds of snow. She was trudging from house to house, pushing through snow as she walked. People reluctantly opened doors that had been blocked by snow. Parents scolded her before she could say anything, saying that she shouldn't be out and to go home. Many people didn't even answer, although they were obviously home.

Eventually a mom answered. Patty meekly asked about her cat. The mom yelled, "Vic, get up here, a girl is here for the cat!" He ran up and reluctantly handed her the cat. They were inseparable from then on. Family dinners, picnics, tied at the hip. Clearly, they were soul mates. Until they each grew apart and somehow, married other people. Then when one became single, the other was still married. Finally, they were both single at the same time. They married and now have three children. She tells the story much better, but the point is that sometimes the path to your soul mate, LTR (Long Term Relationship), or marriage can be a long and winding road, and you have to trudge through a snowstorm. That was way back when—a different time, when dating was much easier and less complicated, and people were happy with one person.

Now, dating is a mixed-up ball of chewing gum, used dental floss, and thorns. You message or text a stranger who you know very little about, but you have some things in common, and they look fairly cute in photos. When you meet in person, you both may be satisfied, or one of you may be disappointed. It is hard to tell what the other person is thinking. Sometimes a guy looks great in person but there is no connection, no spark, no attraction whatsoever. Women know if they want to kiss a guy within the first five seconds of meeting him. Guys come to a date with a fantasy of perfection and are often disappointed. No matter—most guys would still have sex with their dates if the night progressed accordingly. If women are supposed to be able to tell within the first five seconds, I wondered if my chemistry meter was broken. Maybe the guys I didn't like I actually should have liked because they were a good fit for me.

I sometimes wondered if it was similar to my poor sense of direction. If you look up navigationally challenged in the dictionary you'll find a picture of me. My brother teases me: "Whichever way you **think** you should go, always go the other way." So, maybe I should pursue the guys that I'm not attracted to. It's all so confusing. Throwing me further off-course is that at times you have no idea if the guy likes you; he may be keeping his options open by looking for other girls to date, or he could even be actively dating three girls at once.

Women can do this too of course. In the eighties or nineties, dating was more linear. You met someone and dated them and then broke up to date someone else, or moved in together or married them. Dating may be that ball of chewing gum, used dental floss, and thorns, but you have to play to win.

6. To Date or Not to Date?

Dating sometimes gets a bad rap. I guess it depends on one's perspective. My brother absolutely loathes dating. His view of dating is that he takes a girl out, she's judgmental or crazy, then he is left to pay $350 for the experience. He vowed years ago to never date again. He had long-term girlfriends for years at a time and never cheated. A variety of factors kept him from going to the chapel, and he's still single today and pushing sixty. During his illustrious dating career, he went out with girls who drank too much and ended up crying. One invited an elderly man to join their table. Then she and the old man began to argue about politics, religion, and everything else. And if this wasn't miserable enough, my brother ended up paying for the date *and* the old man.

One girl had what's now known as "the jimmy arms." I believe this was from an episode of *Seinfeld*. When he hugged and kissed her goodbye her arms spontaneously took off like a wayward sparrow. He also dated girls who lied: about smoking, about being single, and other lies. I'm not sure what ended his dating career, but he just didn't have great experiences. I'm a fan of dating and bro insists it's because I don't have to pay, and I'm sure there's some truth to that. Often, I didn't feel like going to the trouble of doing my hair, makeup, and nails. Not to mention the need to arrange rides for the kids, someone to stay with them and make them dinner or order pizza. Mostly, though, I would look forward to meeting someone new. Wondering if there would be a connection or spark. I laughed on every date, and I absolutely love one-on-one time. I wondered each time if this guy would be my man. I had hope each time that I would never have to date again. Of course, some guys make you feel beautiful and funny and interesting, and I'm a fan of that too. Sure, maybe they just wanted to get some action, but regardless I rather enjoyed all of it. I'm sure that's why I kept going back for more.

7. A Slow Start

After my marriage broke up, I started slow by gauging interest and contacting past loves via email and messaging. One former love told me, "You have no idea how much I love you . . . but I have a live-in girlfriend." Another refused to see me because he was married and didn't want his wife to get upset—meaning he was still in love with me, of course. Respect.

While dating in my twenties and thirties, so many people set me up on blind dates. Now? Radio silence among my friends and family. I have over 200 cousins and many wonderful friends, so I thought somebody might know someone. Crickets. I realized that the pool is very shallow and most people either don't know any single guys, or they would never want to set me up with the one single guy they know. As one family friend put it, "I know a few, but no way in hell I'd set you up with them!"

Early on, I realized that it wasn't going to be as easy as I had hoped. I was eating words that I carelessly uttered while I was happily married: "If hubs ever leaves me or dies, I will be on a date later that night." LOL. If you are reading this while contemplating a divorce because you think that there are in fact plenty of fish in the sea, PLEASE DON'T leave what you have. I'm here to tell you, there are *not* plenty of other options, unless you are in your twenties or thirties. George Clooney and Brad Pitt are not out there hoping you will date them, no matter how good you look.

It seems like most people who get divorced are either getting out of a bad situation (abuse, drinking, cheating, drugs, gambling), or they have someone else in mind already. The guys who want to be married are married. They may be cheating while married, but they are married. Lots of the guys I dated were players. They were in a long-term relationship, and they realized that it got old, boring, and stale. I met many men who felt like they were just a paycheck and not loved and adored for who they are. The guys out there are mostly looking for something new; they want variety, and they want excitement. I read so many profiles that said, "I am open to anything." In the beginning, I thought, *Wow! They are so accommodating.* I was so NAÏVE! By "open to anything" they didn't mean pasta versus salad for dinner or working around the schedules of lots of kids. "Open to anything" means threesomes, whips, chains . . . They are looking for a sexual dynamo, deviant or group sex.

8. Ladies' Night Out

Do women need an excuse for a ladies' night out (LNO)? There may be no better excuse than that time your husband leaves you and your kids because he needs space. All the while, everyone KNOWS he's leaving you for a younger, childless woman. The marrieds came out of the woodwork to plan ladies' nights out after my life went from enviable to a tragedy overnight. It was the least they could do. Honestly, I had never really been on an LNO during my marriage. Sure, I had gone to the beach with sorority sisters and my amazing VA girlfriends, but I didn't really drink, so I wasn't the best candidate for the LNO.

These LNOs, lunches, and dinners, along with the care, love, and concern shown to me by dear friends and family members, helped me survive that first year and beyond. My close friends would listen to me cry for hours about my lost love. At first, I thought my ex would continue to be a dad. That didn't work out as planned, so my friends and family listened to me lament about how my kids didn't deserve his abandonment. Hours and hours of tears and sorrow. I can never repay them, and I hope to God I never have to. I would often think of Kate Spade. Right around that same time, her husband left her for another woman, and Kate tragically took her own life. A heartbreaking end to an amazing life. My kids didn't understand when adults would only ask them how I was doing and not them because they assumed their dad was being a dad. I knew why; it was because of Kate Spade. The pain and agony is real and intense. You don't know how you will feel until it happens to you. RIP Kate Spade.

My first LNO was to a Mexican restaurant. There were six of us, including my beloved sister. We still laugh heartily about the things that were said at that ladies' night out. I would repeat it, but it's not suitable for print. One of the ladies knew a few single guys, so after a few drinks, she invited one of them to join us. My friend was not subtle at all. After an hour of him being there and I was clearly NOT interested, she kind of shoved us together on a bench. So there I was, newly dumped and trying not to burst into tears at any given moment . . . and I am talking to a single guy. I wasn't sure I even remembered how because it's not really cool as a married mom to converse with guys one-on-one at a party, kid event, and especially not at a dark bar. I was out of practice. This guy, nice enough I am sure, but at age 56, he still lived with his parents and could not afford a pet because they were too expensive. Uh, right then I knew this was not my guy. At one point he turned to talk to someone else, and I looked over to find my HILARIOUS friend making the cut-off sign to her neck, as in DO NOT get involved with this guy! No worries, Mama, I have no intention of ever seeing him again. At the time all I could do was laugh. He wondered what caused my sudden outburst, and I just said, "The moms are hilarious." Later my friend referred to him as "jorts" because he had on cut-off long jean shorts and a muscle shirt. My hilarious friend pointed out that you only wear a muscle shirt if you have muscles!! She basically screamed at the mom who introduced us. That mom responded, "Well, he's single at least?!" My friend yelled, "She's not desperate!!" It was hysterical. I assumed things had to improve from there.

9. My First

You always remember your first. No, not my first time . . . my first date after being married for nearly eighteen years. I was excited. I took a long time to get ready, deciding what to wear on my first date. I sent my Ohio BFF and sister photos: what about this? Does this look better? My first date couldn't have gone better. I do recommend going out with someone you know first, as long as you can accept that it may not be a match. Decide that you are just in it to have some laughs. That really applies to every date. My first was a wonderful, charming, classy, and debonair former co-worker. Let's call him: Yankee Fan. I phoned him after my ex left, because I knew that Yankee Fan had a thing for me. The night of our highly anticipated date, I managed to arrange for all my kids to be away when he picked me up. This has only happened a handful of times in the five years of my dating adventures. Yankee Fan showed up in a car worth more than double my annual salary, and he brought flowers! He was adorable and charming, and we laughed a lot. He was the consummate gentleman and held doors and stood up when I went to the ladies' room.

I am aging myself with this, but I remember a time when gentlemen actually did this and it was flattering. Yankee Fan was very old school and nothing but class. He also spent probably $300 on dinner at Ruth's Chris and didn't think anything of it. Since I was used to pizza places and Chick-fil-A, this was a refreshing luxury. It was a wonderful night, and he set the bar very high. We went out five more times and each time was great; however, I wasn't ready to go all the way. I just wasn't sure. My body had changed since a man other than my ex last saw me naked. Hell, the last time I was naked was in the nineties for God's sake. I was clothed and afraid.

Yankee Fan called one day with news. He said, "I have some news that I want to tell you before you find out from the girls [my VA work friends]." My mind raced, what could it be? During that split second, my imagination went wild. Was he engaged? Did he have cancer? Turns out he had hoped something would work out with me but since I wasn't ready, he decided to move to Spain with his company. I was relieved that he didn't have cancer because so many people in my life at that time had cancer. Timing is everything, and I am sure if he was number 25 in the lineup, we might have been happily coupled up. Honestly, Yankees Fan would have been a great match for me because he has a great sense of humor, a fun lifestyle, and he did not mind that I have what I fondly refer to as "a hundred kids." We do keep in touch, and we might take a trip to Greece in the future. Or he could meet someone and that door would be shut forever. Time will tell.

10. A Facebook match?

I had not yet jumped into the world of online dating but was starting to consider it. I had always wanted to do speed dating where you meet up with twenty-five people in one night, but that had fallen out of fashion, and I think it was intended for the younger people because the elderly pool is too shallow.

One night, a guy dropped into my DMs (I've always wanted to say that). I didn't know him, had never heard of him, but we did have some mutual Facebook friends. He asked me out. Why not? I was game, so we went out on a date. While there, I ran into my kids' dentist (a drop-dead gorgeous woman), who was confused about why we were together because she didn't know that I was divorced. I only discovered this years later. He was an active AA member, so maybe she assumed that we had that in common.

Anyway, the real punchline to this story is that over our wholesome sodas I discovered that he had been married to a friend of mine. In my defense, I had not seen my friend in many years, and he was her second husband. She kept her name, so I had *no idea*. Whoopsie, my mistake. Lucky for me, there was not a connection, so I was not planning on seeing him again. I did have the misfortune of telling my friend when I ran into her at the hair salon. She did not find it as humorous as I had hoped. In fact, she didn't find any humor in it at all—quite the opposite. She turned white with the horrified thought of her evil ex dating her friend. I am sure I would have felt the same way. She had been concerned about my well-being. It took me a while to convince her that I was never going to see him again.

Note to self: find out a little more about people before you go on a date. Happy ending, though, my friend has been happily coupled up for four years and she recently got married. A year or two later, we were at a bar party with about forty people, and he showed up. I grabbed her and said, OMG don't look now but I think that's your ex on a date with an unsuspecting victim. We both laughed and laughed.

11. Scams!!

It is a phenomenon beyond comprehension. I am not sure how or why this happens, but it does, time and again. People willingly give strangers money. On-line suitors whom they have never met and will never meet. Hard-earned money that could be going to pay for retirement, bills, travel, charitable causes. Money is being handed over to criminals daily. Millions and millions of dollars spent on fake profiles.

My number one piece of advice will always be: **do not** give anyone money for any reason.

Repeat after me: I (state your name) will never give anyone money for any reason—ever!

I set out on my dating journey with the mantra that I would not spend any money on guys and not pay for first dates. My reasoning: what little money I had from my meager salary and child support was to be spent on my kids. You can stop reading now because if you don't send guys money and you keep your safety in mind, you will have fun.

Please know that it happens to the smartest, youngest, oldest, and savviest women and men you know. One billion dollars was lost to romance scams in 2024, and the scams are on the rise. What most people don't realize is that it is not actually a crime. People send money and gift cards willingly.

Nobody is stealing from them, unless you consider that they are stealing hearts, hopes, and dreams. I implore you to spread the word because once you discover that your loved one (parent, sibling, friend) is sending money or gift cards to the "love of their life", it is too late to stop them. Another startling fact is that once someone sends money, they are more likely to do it again and again. They actually do it more than once. Seems as though they would learn a lesson, but they don't.

I guess the hope and desire to meet that special someone, leads people to make poor decisions. These criminals video chat with their victims and spend hours and hours texting and reeling them in before they ask for money. Get to know fake profiles from real ones. My sister has been married for 28 years, and she has only looked at some of the dating apps a few times for fun with me. She can spot a fake in two seconds flat. Don't be desperate and blind. Please. Give your money to a charity, not these predators.

HOW TO SPOT A FAKE:

- He is working out of state or overseas but will go out with you when he returns. (This really appeals to people who aren't quite ready to date.)
- He is in the military. (Love military guys, but at our age, they are retired.)
- He lives overseas or is from Poland or Italy or elsewhere.
- He is a widower. (Sorry to those who are, but lots are fake.)

- He only has one photo in his profile, and it's blurry or too professional (pulled from a magazine).
- He wants to use What's App or another alternate messaging platform, other than the dating app.
- He is exceedingly handsome.
- He is going on an overseas business trip
- He has a sick relative who needs money for surgery.
- He lost his wallet in the airport and was detained in Mexico.
- He's instantly in love with you although you've never met.
- He says things you have longed to hear about treating you like a princess.
- He directly or indirectly talks about how wealthy he is, talking about lavish gifts, diamonds and trips he will bestow on you.
- He doesn't ask you out after about a week of texting/ messaging.
- He talks to your family and friends/ seems legit

12. Close to Home

Don't think of the scammers as one person. It can be an actual company or group of people stealing from unsuspecting love interests. It is so convincing because these scammers even FaceTime unsuspecting victims. The logic is that of course they must be real because they are FaceTiming me. It is a network of salespeople selling you the idea of being swept off your feet. They know exactly what to say.

Men seem to get the sick relative, abusive ex, or family poverty type stories. Women tend to meet a wealthy businessman traveling for their job when suddenly their wallet is stolen. A 68-year-old friend was a widow. Her husband of nearly fifty years had been verbally abusive, belittled her, and was just a tough guy to live with in general. She went out with some guys in their late sixties and seventies, and they were on a fixed income, talked too loudly and were disappointing. They were the real deal. Sadly, the real deal isn't what she was hoping for.

Then one day, while she was looking at online profiles, wham! Prince Charming himself showed up as a wealthy Polish businessman living in Miami. He took the time to really get to know her and he seemed to truly appreciate her. He had been looking for someone just like her his whole life.

He wanted to know everything about her. He made her feel young again. They texted, talked, and FaceTimed daily. He was what she had wished to be married to all those painful years. She wanted a do-over, and he was finally here. Of course, he was wealthy and promised to take her on a trip to Hawaii. He also said he would put a big rock on her hand. This went on for several months. Before they had the chance to meet, he had to take a trip to Mexico to close on a lucrative business deal. He messaged her to tell her that someone had stolen his wallet, and he was being detained. He needed money quickly so he could escape. She wired him money. He would pay her back when she picked him up from the airport upon his return. His flight was delayed.

This played out several times. Her daughters asked me to contact her. I did, and although I felt as if my warning message had sunk in, she later became incensed, saying that we would all be sorry when we realized that he was real and was her one chance for true happiness. He would soon sweep her off her feet to a life of wedded bliss and wealth. There was no convincing her that the man of her dreams, the man she had hoped and prayed for, was in fact a scammer. Her family had an intervention.

In the end, she was out $90,000, but she still thought he was real. Many of the people who have been scammed actually still believed the perpetrator was real. When my sister last saw her, she seemed fine. My sister was relieved because she had seemed to move on, until they were getting up to part ways. Our friend nudged her then showed her a photo and said, "I just wanted to show you my new man." My sister's heart sank. It was a picture of a guy who looked like Sean

Connery. My sister made a feeble attempt at a wake up call, "You know, when they look too good to be true, they usually are." Our friend responded, "He FaceTimes me every night." He was number three that we know of.

13. eHarmony?

I wasn't going to be deterred by the fakes. I dipped my toe in and started with some free dating apps. I got burned by guys who canceled before going out: fakes. Then I decided to pay for eHarmony. After weeks on the app, I had not heard from anyone. Hello? Is it me? Why isn't anyone asking me out? There are some apps where guys can't message you unless you message them first. But I had been reaching out to guys. Crickets. Not only was this a huge ego blow, but it was also boring. I was going to quit.

I asked myself: Is this really worth the rejection? What is wrong with me? My Ohio BFF and my sister tried to encourage me, but both were married so they didn't have a clue. "That is ridiculous, you need to try another app! You're gorgeous!" (Ohio BFF is my biggest fan if you couldn't tell). "How about Plenty of Fish?"

"I don't have time for that!" I said. Long story short, Ohio BFF, a stay-at-home mom with grown kids, wanted to prove that I could meet the man of my dreams. She opened an account for me and acted on my behalf. After ten minutes of posting my profile, I had a hundred likes. She was so excited. I have to admit, I was loving it. Sometimes things happen when you least expect it! By *things* I mean more like *a* thing.

In less than forty-eight hours on the app, we received a legendary dick pic! I was driving at the time and she called to tell me. I squealed wheels to pull over and look. It was a head-to-knee photo. I laughed hysterically—could not stop laughing. Not at his physique or size, mind you. The funny thing is that he and Ohio BFF (who he thought was me) were talking about cooking! Making pasta. Right before the dick pic he said something like, "I'd be showing up for dinner like . . ." (insert dick pic). Hilarious. I wasn't sure what to say to the guy afterward because my Ohio BFF insisted that I take over from there. Understandably so, I mean, she is married! He was surprised I wasn't into an unsolicited dick pic and the relationship ended before it began. I thought dick pics would happen more often but my next set was about six years later, following a text about the death of Jimmy Carter?! Again, a totally unrelated topic. I texted one of my guy friends about this to get his take on it and he responded "Nothing comforts after a presidential death like a dick pic!" LOL.

14. The Widower

I met up with an elementary school friend who I had not seen in forty-five years. When I was six, he actually rescued me from nearly drowning. I had fallen into the pool after breaking my arm, then swam to the other side of the pool with one arm. Six-year-old logic, I guess? I had trouble getting out, so he assisted me, then told the lifeguard that I had hurt my arm (I was too shy to tell). He later became an ocean lifeguard and that's how he met his wife. They had been married for about twenty-five years; she was his best friend. In her early forties, she died suddenly, leaving him as a single father of three. It was a heartbreaking end to a beautiful relationship. Their love story would make anyone cry.

I met up with him about five years after she passed. His online dating stories were hysterical, and they gave me insight into the online dating world for men. He went out with several women who had to use a car-installed breathalyzer to start their cars. He went out with someone who brought her three young children and told them to sit in a corner while they sat a few tables away sipping coffee. Needless to say, there were many interruptions. I can relate, sister! (P.S. I never did that.) Several women said they didn't smoke. After a few drinks, they were blowing smoke in his face. Of course, he met up with ladies who were completely unrecognizable from their profile photos. It must be so hard meeting someone when you have been married to the love of your life. I got the feeling that he was about to give up. Finally, he met a beautiful widow, and they recently bought a house and got engaged. They are having a fabulous time, traveling all over on his yacht. They seem to be a great match.

15. The Liar

To be fair, it is hard to tell who lied and who didn't, and many people probably lied about various things. I will never know the extent of the lies, but I know they exist. The liar is surely not alone in his web of lies. Ohio BFF suggested that I should fib on my dating profile using a younger age or just not mention that I have kids, which is hilarious, but I get her point. Nothing attractive about a woman with sole custody of a hundred kids.

I had nothing to hide and felt basically that the dating world should take me or leave me. In retrospect, maybe she was right—who knows? Nonetheless, I had no trouble getting dates.

The Liar was very attractive. A tall, thin, salt-and-pepper distinguished golfer type. The Liar told me he was fifty-four, but he was actually sixty-one. Some people think this is no harm, no foul. Others (my siblings) think it is a big red flag. It didn't bother me that much, but it gave me pause. If he's lying about that, what else is he lying about? Ironically, I would have gone out with him had I known his real age.

I don't think I was what he was looking for. At one point, he kind of said as much: I'm looking for someone with more time on their hands, but I'd like to casually date you. Now those same words would translate into, "I don't see you for a LTR, but you're cute enough to have sex with." Let's face it, what guy is out there right now thinking I would really like to meet a single mom of teenagers with neither money nor time? Most guys are thinking, now that I am finally divorced, I want to have sex with at least fifty random women, then date a woman twenty or more years younger who looks like a supermodel, has plenty of money, doesn't work, and has one grown child, preferably a son.

Getting back to The Liar. This was a classic case of it's not you, it's me. It really was my fault. After five dates, the magic number for taking it to the next level, I just wasn't ready. I was attracted to him, but I couldn't imagine having sex with him. The Liar was temporarily staying in one of the hotels we had stayed in after the house fire, weeks before our marriage imploded. He implied that he lived in a townhouse, but he was living in that seedy hotel while the townhouse was being built. (The siblings count that as lie number 2, btw.) Anyway, for whatever reason, it creeped me out, the thought of having sex in THAT hotel. Obviously, my house was not an option for sex because my kids are ALWAYS home. He also had a tick—not terrible but he blinked both eyes from time to time in a nervous manner. Sorry, was that mean? Our dates went from romantic and fun to him wanting to analyze why I didn't want to have sex. It just wasn't meant to be. I had to let him go. I ran into the Liar two years later at a bar. Ohio BFF just happened to be in town for the ill-fated meeting. I had spotted him and was contemplating a dodge, but there was no way out. I tried to introduce him to Ohio BFF, but she fled to the gift shop before I could say anything. He patted me on the arm as if I was terminally ill and said "How are youuuu?" with the sad eyes. I responded with "great!" wondering why the pity party. Then cutting me off mid sentence, he told me that he was engaged to a younger woman. They wear it like a badge of honor. LOL, congrats Liar, I wish you two the best. Sidenote: I still didn't want to have sex with him.

16. Tattoo Sleeves

Sometimes in the planning process for a pre-date or date, things get rescheduled. Tattoo Sleeves and I had made a few attempts to meet and finally set a date to meet at a quaint little coffee shop. Coffee dates are my least favorite, but it tends to be a quick and easy way to determine if you want a real date. I was already in the parking lot when he texted to cancel. Ugh. I had to take off work to meet him. Thanks a lot, Tattoo Sleeves.

After I told him I was already there, he decided to show up. This guy was exciting. He wasn't anyone's garden variety middle-aged bachelor. Nothing about him was typical. He was a fifty-year-old rock star. Literally. He was in several bands and was also a teacher at one of my kids' schools. We chatted for a while, and he told me stories about being in bands and wild escapades. I think he was gauging my sexability? It was an hour-long date, and we laughed and flirted. We were the only people in the coffee shop so that was nice. Nothing worse than knowing people are analyzing your first date banter. He walked me to my car, and we had a romantic embrace and passionate kiss during one of those spontaneous summer rainstorms. The last thing he said was, "We are going to have a lot of fun together!" He was not interested in marriage, and neither was I. We texted often; some were steamy, which was a lot of fun.

The perceived conflict of him working at my kid's school bothered him immensely. I get it: he didn't want to risk a great job for a piece of ass. I told my kid after graduation. He was beyond thrilled. At that point I hadn't seen Tattoo Sleeves in many years. Still, my eighteen-year-old was so excited that he begged me to let him tell his friends, teachers, and classmates. I wasn't prepared for this reaction because this was a kid who didn't want me to date. I guess things change when your mom dates someone "so dope." My kid insisted that I text him in an attempt to rekindle, which I did. By then, Tattoo Sleeves had forgotten who I was. The nerve! Then major disappointment set in when my kid realized that Tattoo Sleeves was not going to be his new stepdad.

17. Unrecognizable

Ladies, please display a variety of profile photos, some showing the REAL you, so that your dates will be able to recognize
you when they see you. Yes, we all looked a lot better twenty
or thirty years ago but displaying misleading photos is a bad
idea. This is the number one complaint from every single guy
I dated about the online dating racket. In case you haven't
noticed, most guys care a lot about looks. Guys are shallow,
or rather, they are visual. This doesn't change when they turn
fifty or sixty. In fact, it may even become even worse as they
age. Wouldn't you rather have them pleasantly surprised than
disappointed? One guy told me: you are much hotter in person
than you are in your photos. This is the response you should
strive for, ladies. I should have married him on the spot! And
for God's sake, no Instagram cat or bunny ear photos. As one
guy put it, "Ladies, I am not trying to date a cartoon puppy!"

Unrecognizable was actually a lot better looking in person than he was in his photos. He was even taller, if that
makes sense. Guys typically lie about height if they are under
six feet. Five ten is actually five eight, and so on. We were
meeting for lunch. I walked into the little diner, smiled at the
handsome guy in the doorway, and then looked around at all
the tables. He kind of chuckled and said my name. "Oh my

gosh!" I exclaimed. "You are so much more attractive in person. I mean you looked good in photos, but wow!" He seemed flattered. So, it turned out that he was stopping in for lunch with me then heading down South because his "Pop" was dying. He teared up a bit as he talked about his beloved father. I felt for the guy because I'm sure he had not planned on crying on a lunch date. He wouldn't be the last guy who cried on a date with me, though, I'm sorry to report. I must bring it out in them.

I hugged and kissed him goodbye but never heard from him again. Dating is sometimes like waitressing. When you get a bad tip, you can't tell whether the people were cheap or if they thought the service was bad. That is why I always tip well. If I have a serious concern, I tell the manager. Ghosting is to be expected in the wild, wild world of dating. I did not let it bother me. I have more important things to worry about, like raising a hundred kids and my next date. Not sure what happened with Unrecognizable. We will never know for sure.

18. Always a Cereal Dater

When I think back to dating in my twenties and thirties, I realize that I was a cereal dater then too. I never wanted to be, but things never quite worked out for me. There was my high school boyfriend—loved him and would sneak out at night to walk three miles to his house. My first love had a problem with lying and once I went to work at a pool and he was holding hands with another girl. Of course, I started dating him again in college after he rode a moped to come see me. A three-hour drive that probably took six hours on the moped. . . . Ah, youth. He was a waiter last I heard, and I recently stalked him on Facebook to see him with his wife and two kids.

From there, I dated a couple other guys in college: a dependable guy and a rugby player. I probably should have married the dependable guy, but the world was calling, and I had to answer that call. Incidentally, I ran into the rugby player one day, post-college, walking through the quaint town of Annapolis. He was with a hot girl, and I was licking an ice cream cone. Uh, not exactly the chance meeting dreams are made of, but these things happen. I was mortified but acted confident as I tried to compose myself and lick the ice cream from all over my mouth. Dependable college guy is happily married to an adorable lady, and they have one child who attends our alma mater. It makes me happy to see their posts on Facebook. Alas, a little sigh of regret creeps in sometimes.

During my career working for the military, I dated too many guys to count. Not because I really wanted to, but because I had to find the one, and it took time. Sometimes I'd meet a guy, fall madly in love, and then he'd leave for another duty station. I broke hearts along the way, but I had my heart broken many times as well. There are several guys that I should have married, and then there were those who I absolutely shouldn't have gone on a second date with.

Some of the "shouldn't haves" made my friends and family scratch their heads with dismay. One such guy I met overseas. He smoked like a chimney and drank at least six beers a day. Not really my kind of guy, but there was something about him. Maybe it was the 6'4" height and washboard stomach? Then there was a Special Forces guy who I dated for a year, and he never touched me—not once. You're probably thinking that he's gay, but he wrote to me years later to let me know he had married a female Army officer. There was a lot of drama and trauma surrounding my relationships and I often couldn't decide between two guys. Or rather, I'd be dating one but missing another one. I'm sure it was the hurt-or-be-hurt mentality. I went through this for ten years before finally settling down. Sometimes therapy takes time to sink in, but I know now that it's me. I take full responsibility for my cereal dating, then and now.

19. The Hidden Gem

Hidden Gem was so kind. I had been on a roll, and he was the third guy I had met up with that week. Again, some dates were just a quick lunch during camp or a drink during soccer practice. I made time for my plethora of men while driving my hundred kids all over the place and working full-time. If I can make time, anyone can.

I don't like to drink and drive so I either had one drink or friends drove me, or I Ubered. He was short and adorable. He said, among other sweet things: "Your ex must be crazy to have let you go." This is the reason we date. Because sometimes a stranger can really make a difference in our lives, and he probably has no idea of the impact these words had on me. Thank you, Hidden Gem, I couldn't agree more. I loved my ex with all my heart, and I miss what we had. I would have done anything for him and to keep our family together but he rejected me and our perfect life. It helps to get reassurance from men sometimes that you are still valuable. I recently went back to the place where I met Hidden Gem, and I thought about him fondly. He is out there and he has no idea how much our date and his kind words meant to me. Even if he was just trying to get laid, albeit unsuccessfully.

20. The Towels

Sometimes you know it's not a match but at least you have some laughs and get a great story out of the date. I enjoy men, and I really hadn't talked to any for eighteen years, so I was enjoying it immensely and didn't care if it turned into anything more. I had just been to divorce court, and I Ubered to a date, which was very empowering, I must say.

This guy had been married to a gorgeous woman who was very controlling. As I like to say, most men prefer a hot skinny woman who is batshit crazy to an average-looking normal one. They get themselves into these situations because they place looks above everything else. He had taken a new job and wanted to play golf during his interim week. He knew she would be mad, so he didn't tell her about his week off. He claims he wasn't cheating but she had him followed and saw he was playing golf, shooting hoops, fishing, going to bars, and enjoying life . . . without her. She kicked him out. This was right before everyone started using Find my Friends and Life 360. Those apps are a cheater's nightmare and conversely, a controlling person's dream. He mostly talked about how gorgeous his crazy wife was and had to fight the urge to show me a photo.

He did tell me a funny story, though. He had season tickets to the Ravens games. Their arch-rival is the Steelers, and the fans bring yellow towels, "terrible towels," to ferociously swing around OUR stadium. Great for them, but so annoying for the rest of us. In his section, they have a hard-and-fast rule: NO TOWELS! He and his friends would grab the towels out of people's back pockets and watch them look around for their beloved towel. They confront towel wielders announcing that "we don't do that here" while holding out a hand (as in, give me your towel). The confused Steelers fans point to other sections of the stadium where the towels are flying freely. He tells them, "Yes, there (pointing upward), but not here (pointing downward and shaking his head)."

He explained that teamwork makes the dream work and that the whole section takes part. He has escaped some near brawls. He does return the towels to the fans after the game, so he says. I assume he went back to his gorgeous, controlling wife. I hope they live happily ever after.

21. Feelings

I don't think of myself as emotional. I can't remember ever crying during my eighteen years of marriage. I am kind of tough in that way, and I have learned that relationships sometimes require being vulnerable and emotional. That said, I have lots of female friends, and they are emotional. They will cry at movies, even commercials. They cry when they're angry. They cry when they have their periods. I get it, girls cry and it's okay. In our fifties, we have mostly grown out of game playing, grudge holding, jealousy, etc. I try not to participate in any of that, but I do have feelings. I was very optimistic about who might be out there waiting in the wings for me while still hurting from the rejection.

There are all kinds of scenarios, but chances are that you weren't planning on being in this on-line dating situation years prior to being here. I was full of hope in the beginning, and it has waned over the years. That same little girl who was doodling hearts and writing her name with her sixth grade crush's last name is now an old, divorced lady, but those feelings are still there. It's how we were raised; it's our society. A high value is placed on marriage and coupling, and people feel sorry for you when you're single. Maybe some marrieds secretly covet your lifestyle, but mostly they love you and wish you could meet a nice man. There is a perception that there is a 50% divorce rate, but the singles of our generation usually get remarried. If I had a dollar for every married person who thinks everyone is single, I would be a millionaire. Truth is most people are part of a couple.

It is easy to get caught up in fantasies of a life together while reading profiles. It goes something like this: he looks cute; aw, he caught a big fish; we both have teens. What?! He loves Swedish fish, he loves the movie that I love, we like the same sports teams, he shops at Costco too! He is PERFECT! You send him a short message. Maybe even makes a joke related to his profile. You excitedly anticipate his response. You keep checking. Maybe he was busy. You check again. Maybe he was traveling. A week goes by, and Mr. Perfect sadly never responds to your message. After a week, he is not going to. My brother faced this time and again, and he is a very attractive guy. He would take the time to comb through profiles and comment on things that seemed important to his potential dates. Most of them would never write back. He gave up altogether, which is a shame because he is a proverbial catch, great-looking and fun.

My advice is to reach out to a lot of guys and try not to get caught up on any of them. Then message, text, or talk to several at once and maybe go on three quick dates in a week or so. This way you spread out your emotions over three guys instead of just one. All your emotional eggs are not in one basket. Dating is different now and you must respond accordingly. When and if you meet a guy who you want to see exclusively, you can give up on the other guys. I admit in the beginning I was writing my name with his fake last name and imagining our life together. This makes it difficult to evaluate the guy objectively and harder to move on when it doesn't work out. When you are looking at guys' profiles, just scroll through like online shopping. Choose all different guys or one type, but choose a lot of them. Some guys might have a height restriction or hate your name or don't date blonds or women with kids. Who knows? Don't take it personally. Keep the emotions out of the process as much as possible.

22. The Police Officer

I guess it's no secret that some professions breed cheaters. I worked for the military, so I was familiar with the frequency of infidelity. Men working in the military tend to get restless, especially when on deployments. They are hunkered down in bunkers, risking their lives, and defending our freedom. They could literally die at any moment. Do you think this is why they cheat? Maybe it's because most women cannot resist a man in uniform. In any case, they are known to stray. I've learned over the years that the other cheating professions are attorneys, pilots, firemen, and police officers. Maybe it is because they have plenty of opportunities with their crazy schedules. Do you think it is a kind of peer pressure, an acceptable norm? Knowing about these cheating professions, I tiptoed into my date with the Police Officer.

I was at the beach with my family. We were sitting under umbrellas just chatting and enjoying the beautiful Frisco beach in North Carolina. I think everyone was surprised that I had not met Mr. Right part 2 by that point so my brother decided to take charge and grabbed my phone to peruse the options.

After a lot of laughter, head shaking, and swiping left, he came to his perfect choice for me. "Here he is—THIS is the one!" The police officer's profile was full of patriotic photos and memes. "Right here," he said, pointing to his profile. "This is who you need to date." Then he handed the phone back to me. His work was done. Considering that my own dating choices hadn't really worked out too well, I decided what the hell? and I reached out to him. After messaging back and forth a few times, he wanted to talk—as in, talk on the phone.

I'm not a fan of phone conversations in general. Once a guy called me and without saying hello, he started having phone sex. All I could do was laugh, and he actually got mad so I hung up. That was our first and last conversation. I had a few who got off on talking to an unsuspecting middle-aged woman about sex. I never actually met any of them. I'm sure they were married and just wanted to whack off. That's not cheating, right? Just kidding, I'd say it is, but my views on cheating have changed over the years. I truly admire people who stay in marriages during and after cheating. Yes, it is ideal not to cheat but lots of people do and they keep their families intact.

Anyway, the police officer wanted to talk, so I obliged. His voice was okay, and he was a real chatty Kathy. His sister and mother had recently passed away from cancer within months of one another. I felt so bad for him. He had been married twice, but had only one kid. He had been in the military, had a motorcycle, he seemed like a fun guy. We met in the city because he was coming from the north. He pulled into the parking lot and I immediately knew that he wasn't my guy. He had horribly crooked teeth. It was distracting. Yes, now I sound shallow, but I'm just being honest. You don't

see that with the Millennials or Gen Zs, but back in the sixties and seventies, parents couldn't always afford braces. Now
braces are mainstream; it is rare to meet a kid who didn't have
braces.

Some people meet a person, know they aren't attracted
to them at first sight, and turn around and leave. I'm not that
person. I hugged him and we went inside, then kissed at the
table. LOL, I sound like a ho now, but it is pertinent to the
story. The waitress came over mid-kiss. Somehow, she and I
started talking about our seventeen-year-old sons. We laughed
about how they hoard cups and plates, play video games, and
have started calling us "bruh" instead of Mom. Then she said
her son was probably the reason she was still single. I guess
the police officer felt left out because without skipping a beat,
he piped in, "I'm single too," then he laughed. She said something like, "Alrighty then," and left to get our drinks. It was
an odd thing for him to say because she had seen us kissing
just minutes prior. I am sure she didn't know how to respond.

The date went on, we kissed again, and laughed. At one
point he moved very close to my face and asked, "Well, do
you like me?" I answered, "Yes, of course!" Meanwhile, inside
I was thinking, *weirdo, definitely not going to go out with him
again*. At the end of dinner, we got up from the table and
started walking toward the door. He said, "Watch this, I'm
going to ask the waitress for her number." I said okay, not
caring at all, trust me, and I proceeded to walk to the door. I
paused at the door. I heard an emphatic "absolutely!" from the
waitress. He then caught up to me and asked why I left. I said
I didn't want to make her feel bad. Then I asked if he got her
number and he said, "Aw no, I was just kidding!" We parted

ways and afterward he texted me to see when we could go out again. Hard pass, officer.

23. Dowdy

For the record, I had a good time on every single date. Every guy I went out with was kind, generous and worthy of love. I wish all of them the very best.

Dowdy was one of the rare guys I dated who could be Googled. He was connected and extremely handsome in his profile pictures. Picture a tall dark and handsome movie star. In the beginning, I was either super paranoid or thorough, depending how you look at it. I would research guys based on their phone numbers. I think this one mentioned what he did, so I Googled it, and he came right up.

He was very impressive online and never married, no kids. Turns out that's not always a plus. No kids isn't the picnic I expected because kids are common ground, although more so when you're in a moms group. Honestly, I don't want to talk about my kids while dating. I will, but I'd rather not. I was dating to get away from that chaotic part of my life.

Most of the guys I met had kids, but the moms were doing the majority of the child-rearing, driving, and appointments, and the Dad was just showing up once a week or weekends— which is more participation than my kids had. The dads were free to travel, date, work, and basically do whatever they wanted, while the moms were carrying the heavy load. There are exceptions but this seemed common. Most of the guys I dated had college age kids or older though.

Dowdy was very interesting. He lived with a lady for five years. She left her kids to move in with him. He went on to tell me that she had major emotional issues, and he had to let her go. Wow, you don't say, Dowdy? Probably the only time I gave a date unsolicited advice. I couldn't resist: Don't date a mom who leaves her kids. Dowdy was nice enough and well-educated, but unfortunately, those movie star photos couldn't capture the all-out dorky way he walked. I'm sorry, but Dowdy walked like a grandpa. We hugged goodbye and he implored me to keep in touch because he wanted to see how my life turns out, ironically pertaining to the kids. I never heard from Dowdy again.

24. Catholic Guy

On the way to a date with Catholic Guy, I was chatting with my next date, Hot AF. Maybe that wasn't fair, but I was definitely distracted by the excitement brewing from just talking to Hot AF, although he lived far away and I was hoping to meet someone local.

As usual, I met Catholic Guy in the parking lot. I recognized his car from the high school sticker on the back. Our kids had gone to the same school. Catholic Guy's wife was a drug addict, leaving him with two children. He seemed like a fabulous dad, which was an attractive feature. He was chatty, which honestly is more fun than a painfully quiet man.

Once, while living in poverty in the paradise that is Coronado in my premarital days, I asked a neighbor over for dinner. He did not say two words during our short time together. Trying to get him to answer a question was like pulling teeth. Do you have siblings? "Two." Are you close to them? "No." What do you do for the military? "Secret stuff." After an hour of this painful experience, he decided to speak, and I was super-excited. He broke through the shy phase and was finally going to say something! He blurted out, "So, do you want to have sex?" I choked on the air. Uh, EXCUSE ME? I don't think I heard you. What did you say? Again, do you want to have sex? After I recovered from the shock, I came up with a response. "Aw, thanks for the offer, but I need to finish up some laundry and call my mom" (to tell her about my ludicrous dinner guest). Then he followed that up with: "Well, I normally get a very positive response from that question." Really? Women have sunk to the level where they will have sex with a guy who can't form sentences? Buh-bye, neighbor dude.

Now, Catholic Guy would NEVER have said something like that. He talked about how repulsed he was when women suggested a one night stand. His stories were interesting. He talked 99.9% of the time. Afterward, he said (and this sums up men well): "We really had a great connection; I'd love to see you again." Lots of guys (and probably girls) feel connected after they talk nonstop about themselves. If you're shy or don't know what to say on dates or at parties, just ask people questions. Catholic Guy followed that revelation by saying, "Remember tomorrow is a holy day of obligation. Make sure you and the kids go to church." Excuse me? Catholic Guy, please pray for me because I'm out.

25. Swipe Left/Delete

Maybe I'm not the best one to offer advice on choosing dates. As I mentioned before, I did have fun on all the dates, and I never feared for my safety, so there's that.

Well, that's not entirely true. Due to my obsession with *Dateline* type shows, I did worry that my ex would hire one of these guys to kill me. Other than that, I felt 100% safe. I only left one date early, and that was just because I didn't like where it was going. The date was getting really drunk (See the "Oh No" chapter).

At first, you may find yourself combing through profiles and considering each one with a fine-toothed comb. I know girls who do a thorough, and I mean FBI-level, profiling of a guy, before she will even meet him for coffee. I don't have time for that, and I really don't care. You may be the type to swipe left or delete based on the photo, without even reading. You will notice that, unlike girls, guys cannot take a photo. They take selfies from weird angles and look angry in most of their photos. It is comical at times. Next time you're at happy hour with a bunch of marrieds, pull out your dating app and they will have a field day perusing dating options. If nothing else it will make them appreciate what they have.

Conversely, girls' photos are almost too good because girls display their best photos. Women are not going to submit their worst photos because they have already been deleted. So, it seems, many of us are unrecognizable from the photos we submit on dating profiles, in person. This can be a disaster, so again try to keep it real.

Eventually, I started eliminating profiles based on a variety of factors. Location. Geographically undesirable. This is a non-issue for younger people, but I hate night driving, and I have a hundred kids, so if you live an hour away, you are not Mr. Right. If I don't recognize the town name, I'm deleting you. If you look angry in your photo: delete. If you are too short: delete. I have dated short guys, and they are people too, but I am generally more attracted to big guys. If you are a Pens fan: delete. If you look too good: delete. If you are atheist: delete. If you look arrogant: delete. If you want kids: delete. If you like to go antiquing: delete. If you only have one photo: delete. If you have never been married: delete. If you're a widow, sorry but: delete. If you don't have kids: delete. In the beginning, I thought this would be a perfect fit for me, but as the saying goes, "The best parent is the one who doesn't have kids." This is so true. I mean, guys can't relate to moms, but someone who never had kids, nah. I don't want someone judging me because my parenting went from strict to permissive. I was just trying to survive.

Back to my delete list. If someone had sole custody of kids: DELETE! I know that seems contradictory, but seriously, why would I date someone who also has their kids 24/7? I have kids, so the last thing I want to do is date a guy with 24/7 custody of young kids. I know lots of my dates heard my story and wanted no part of me or my life. I can hear them telling their friends now:

"Man, she was cute and fun but she has her kids 24/7: NO THANKS!."

During the 2020 election, many profiles included political preferences. "If you voted for Trump, we are not a match," or the reverse as well. I don't want to date someone who doesn't want to date someone based on political preferences. The point is, that after a while, you know what you can and can't tolerate and what has (and has not) worked for you. You must develop a system of elimination. Guys are doing this too. Some guys like huge boobs, so they would delete me. Maybe they prefer brunettes, or short girls, or girls with only one child. Girls with makeup. A guy once told me that he wanted to date me because I didn't wear makeup. This is hilarious because I do, but had posted photos without makeup as well. Just to keep it real. The point is, don't take it personally if your profile has been rejected. Or if a guy stops texting you, or never asks you out again. It happens to the best of us.

26. Hot AF

Ahhh . . . chemistry! There you are, you sneaky devil. Hot AF was newly divorced because like a lot of the guys I dated, his wife no longer wanted to have sex. Hot AF was so much fun to text with and talk to. He was a man's man but also smart and sexy. He was an executive type from Jersey, but he was living in Texas. We had lots of fun before the date texting about our opposing sports teams.

We met at a local bar on the water. In person, he was fun, attractive. He took charge and ordered food. We made out by the boats. It was steamy; the connection was on fire. I would stare at him, and at one point he said, "You are not listening to a word I'm saying." And I said, "Nope." I couldn't concentrate. During those early dating days, I would have friends Uber me to dates and then pick me up. I called my friend and told her not to get me, that I would drive home with Hot AF. More making out in my neighbor's yard because it was a vacant house at the time. It was fun; there were fireworks and there was also laughter.

I might have had sex but didn't. Not in a guy's truck—wasn't I better than that? Not to mention old? I didn't thankfully, because after our date, I was giddy for days. I knew it wasn't going to be a long-term thing, but still I fantasized about him. Stupid girl-type fantasies like being a couple, not hot sex fantasies, although I was planning on engaging in that eventually.

We were supposed to have another date about two hours from my town, but he was "in the ER with a heart issue." He even sent a photo. Probably a lie. I was disappointed but not devastated because I was dating up a storm at that point. We continued to text on and off for years just about our dating adventures, sports, sex. I hadn't heard from him in a while and then he popped up under a different name on a dating app. I sent him a text with that new name. He was a player and possibly still married. We still texted on and off especially when his teams lost. I just heard from him recently because his team was in the Super Bowl. He's still fun to text with, but it's unlikely I'll ever see him again.

27. Spy Guy

Spy Guy worked for a top-secret US organization, allegedly. He was a lot of fun on the phone. He made me laugh, and I really looked forward to talking to him. Sometimes you just connect over the phone and text. We had a great time, and I looked forward to hearing from him. He had been married to a foreign woman who left him for another guy, and since they didn't have kids, he was ready to move on too. I think it took a while for us to meet up because of my crazy schedule. We talked and texted for a few weeks. He tried to reschedule the date, but I wouldn't let him because I didn't want the anticipation to go on any longer.

We met the night that Abu Bakr al-Baghdadi was taken out by Special Forces and Spy Guy had something to do with that (so he says). Something about surveillance, and he used the name Mr. Green Chip instead of the terrorist's real name. The story could have been made up, who knows? Honestly, he wasn't bad looking, but he looked *a lot* older in person than in the photos, and there was just zero chemistry. He was not very nice to the waiter and that is a **huge** turnoff for me. As interesting as the story was, immediately my dreams were dashed of him being my man.

Spy Guy is the reason I refuse to spend hours texting and talking before meeting. Sometimes the person is vastly different from who you thought they were (which could be said about my ex too, LOL). You must experience this for yourself to fully understand it, but I'd rather you didn't because it is self-defeating and kind of sad. Chemistry can't be determined over the phone. You have to meet in person—and the sooner, the better.

28. Meh?

Some people you meet and you think this could go either way. But then they aren't knocking my socks off with their conversational skills or stories. Meh was a divorced dad whose daughter lived with him. I am not sure why, but I prefer a boy dad to a girl dad. Meh was a bit Guido-ish—Italian and he wore a thick gold necklace. I'm sure you know the type. He was somewhat refined, though. He never made me laugh, which was a minus for sure. If you can't make me laugh or smile in the first hour, I am probably not attracted to you. It felt more like a job interview.

Side note: If you are not going to order food on a date, I am not going to like you. Even if I'm not hungry, it is the gesture that is attractive. That's what I like in a man. Confident, take-charge, generous, and word to the wise, please feed me. Meh basically told me that he was looking for someone with more time on their hands and I wasn't the right fit for the job (of dating him). I really couldn't argue with him, it was true. I really didn't have any time to date a guy who couldn't make me laugh and didn't want to feed me. I thanked him, then left to pick up a kid from practice. I never heard from or saw him again, like the majority of my dates. You have to kiss a lot of frogs.

29. The Handyman

I went out with the Handyman to a local restaurant, and we sat at the bar. Before my dating adventures, I had never sat at a bar. It is a guy thing. He was really tall, which I am a huge fan of. Apparently, I am not the only one because guys often make a comment in their profiles about height such as, "I'm six feet tall because apparently that matters." This makes me giggle a little because in a sense, I'm glad guys are getting a taste of their own medicine.

I had a great time with The Handyman. He was attractive in a respectable, cute way. He asked me out again, but I was busy, and I put him on the back burner. Several months later, I decided to give him another try. He was a devoted dad to his two step kids, who were in their twenties. He seemed like a good guy. He lived thirty minutes away, which is no big deal for the rest of the world, but for me it was hard juggling dating, driving my kids around, and being there for them.

We took walks during one of my kid's practices. Not near the practice, by the way. I had a strict no-meeting-the-kids rule. In fact, I would tell the kids I was going out with my friend or my sister, who would drive me to my dates and pick me up. God love them. This also provided my family with an added layer of safety. They knew where I was going and when

I left. The kids did not need to get their hopes up or in some cases fears tied to my dating escapades and mishaps. Some of my kids wanted me to marry the first guy who came along, while others were nervous about me dating strangers for fear that I would be "mom-napped." I felt like after all they had been through, I should keep it under wraps for the time being.

I envy parents with shared custody primarily because the kids have two parents who love them enough to focus solely on them and make them feel like nothing else matters in the world. I'm also jealous because the fifty-fifty parents get coveted time without the kids. It certainly makes it much easier to date. Shared custody parents could be having an all-out orgy, and their kids would never know because they are gone half the time. The Handyman had not been the primary breadwinner in his marriage. This could have been what led him to being financially unstable, but he was also cheap. I was not sure I could get past that. His handyman skills were very attractive, though, and he was in the process of remodeling his house. I admired the work he had done. I started to think about remodeling one of my bathrooms and how fun it would be to do it together. Hell, I would have settled for him to nail some of my fence posts back on.

I decided to bring him to dinner with my sister and brother-in-law to watch a playoff game. I ran into some of my cousins there as well and they excitedly ran over to meet my date. I would have liked to preface the introduction with a "This is not going to be my boyfriend so don't get excited." Our team was losing (once again), which dampened the mood. We decided to leave. It would have been a nice gesture of The Handyman to pay, but we knew that wasn't going to happen so my generous brother-in-law paid. A few weeks later my BIL told me that The Handyman was "kind of weird." That settled it. Next!

30. Nats Fan

The night the Washington Nationals won the World Series, I went on a date and we watched the game from our table. It was a sports bar right near Nat's stadium and the momentum was exciting. Everybody there had a Nat's shirt on. I had to borrow one from one of my kids. Nat's Fan was short and cute and drove an expensive car. Everyone I have dated owned a more expensive car than my light-blue sore thumb of a mom-mobile.

Nat's fan was married with three young kids. All was going very well in his world. He had just gotten a lucrative promotion and was in the process of building his dream mega-mansion. His wife, a stay-at-home mom, suddenly decided that she wanted to take the kids and move back to her childhood town, which was eight hours away. Who knows what else was going on there? As usual, I only heard one side of the story. No matter what happened, this guy went to visit his kids every weekend and sometimes during the week. He drove eight hours to see his kids. I rather liked that about him, but I wasn't too keen on him talking about money and the fact that he had a lot of it. After the Nats beat the Houston Astros in game 7 of the world series, we high fived everyone and walked out to our cars. A light rain was falling and we kissed under my umbrella, which was rather romantic. He texted me the next day. I would have gone out with him again so I was excited. He just wanted to know if I would come to his place to hook up. Uhhh . . . really? No thanks Nat's fan.

31. Naked and Afraid

One of the hardest parts about dating in your fifties is getting your much older, thicker, more wrinkled self out there again. Just getting out of yoga pants and going on dates can be daunting, but sex, being fully naked? Yikes! In the beginning, I would try on three or four outfits and send photos to my sister and bestie and they would choose. Yes, I was still clothed and afraid, but I wanted sex to be a part of my life. Most guys seem to prefer a confident, body-positive and sex-positive person to someone who complains about how skinny she used to be. I guarantee nobody wants to hear about how you need to lose weight and what kind of diet you are on. Despite what I have said about guys being shallow, personality does matter, and most guys just want to have fun. Still, the thought of a guy seeing me naked again for the first time is terrifying. I cringe as I write this now. Even the most perfect, gorgeous fifty-year-olds are apprehensive. I will admit a little alcohol can help ease the pain of being naked and afraid. Warning though not too much, for me anyway.

Adding to my fears was the fact that I had what the medical community clinically referred to as dyspareunia. Simply stated, I had pain during sex. It was very painful. Not painful as in "it's too dry and you just need some lube," but painful, like, it felt as if a penis would no longer fit. When my marriage was falling apart, I was desperate to cure this. I just assumed that the pain was a side effect of the dreaded menopause. Turns out that it was not a hormonal problem. It felt like a muscular issue. It was hard to describe. I went to the gynecologist, and she just told me to use a lubricant. I was hoping for a hormone patch. I was getting nowhere. I decided to jump ship and go to another doctor. This one was young. She had just had a baby. She told me that based on my symptoms, I needed to go to physical therapy. Pardon me? A what? I basically laughed at her and said no way in hell, thinking wow she is way too young to practice medicine. She wrote me a prescription, but I told her that I was never going to use it. My curiosity took over and I decided to Google it. The first article in the search was a young twenty-something girl describing exactly what it felt like for me to have sex. Turns out dyspareunia can occur at any age, in all body types and situations. In my case, they think it was due to my C-sections. Basically, the muscles were spasming and that was what was making having sex so painful.

Seems like right after I say "I would never", I end up eating those words. I decided to give physical therapy a try. It took me several months to find a provider. It is a specialized field, pelvic floor physical therapy. Basically, there are three rings inside the vagina and the therapist pressed on various areas of the vagina with a wand. I was supposed to do it at home, but who has time for that? Plus, my kids and their friends routinely walk in on me, so I was worried about that happening during the "wanding," LOL. Through the process of going to PT, I learned a lot about the vagina. Some women always have pain during sex, and they just think it is supposed to feel that way because everyone tells them that it hurts the first time. They go their whole lives with this pain, and they think it's normal. WOW. If they would go to PT, they could have pain-free sex. The main takeaway for me from going to PT was that women should only urinate every two hours. I think that is what cured me. I work from home, so I went every time I had the urge. After telling the kids when they were little to "go now" for fear that there wouldn't be a bathroom at the playground, I took my own bad advice too. Eventually I was cured, but who knew for sure because by the time I finished, my husband had left so I had not had sex. So, in addition to the body image struggle, I worried about the pain. Incidentally, my ex paid for every cent of the PT sessions, which was really the least he could do. In essence, his hard-earned money went toward me being able to have amazing sex with other men. Thanks, ex, I appreciate it! One ladies' night out, we promptly toasted to this, and it still makes me laugh. Cheers to pain-free sex!

32. Wine, Please!

Ah, Number 17. He was a maker of wine. He had all the equipment in his basement and hosted wine clubs. Wow! A genius way to meet women, right? (I'm the only woman on earth who doesn't like wine, so it was lost on me.) Married twice and two sons. One in the military and one my son's age.

We met for a romantic dinner. Wine Please was so handsome and said all the right things. He was dreamy. We sat next to a lacrosse team of young teenage boys. Afterward, we kissed, then my friend picked me up. He texted, "When can I see u again?" Hilarious coincidence that when I got his text it came up as Baseball Coach?! My heart skipped a beat. Was it just a glitch in the phone? My son quit playing baseball because of a really mean coach. Oh no, was that coach, Wine Please? I wasn't sure if I should say something. For now, I would just let it lie.

Our second date was wonderful. He was soft spoken and articulate, but fun. I went to his house and we danced. I was so comfortable with him. Next we went on a romantic winery tour. He treated me like a lady, and I loved being with him. He wasn't a fan of texting but in person he was great.

Finally I brought up the coaching thing. Turns out he *was* my son's baseball coach, seven years prior. Thankfully he wasn't the mean coach. Nothing like your kid cock-blocking your chance at happiness because he thought someone was mean when he was probably just a great coach, and my kid wanted to quit.

On the fifth date, it was time, I decided to go all the way. I was scared. My body has changed since the last time, some 20 years ago. Yikes. It had changed a lot, and not like one of those mom-bod-turned-fitness-girl transformations. I wasn't sure if I should but it felt right. He was surprised. "You do, really? Hold on, let me take a shower."

LOL, WHAT?! *Great, more time to feel insecure about my body.* Turns out . . . he was amazing! I left there thinking, Wine Please is my guy. I had finally found him, and in fewer than the twenty dates that my friend said it would take. I'm an overachiever.

The following Friday, we made plans for him to come over to my house at 2:30 then go to happy hour. This was not easy to arrange. I had to summon friends to pick kids up from school and take them to other places. I was nervously excited. But it was three o'clock and he wasn't here. Then 3:15. Then 3:30. I was left to wonder if he didn't like the sex. Was it my body? At nearly 4:30, he texted that he was tied up at work and asked me to come over to his house, which was forty-five minutes away. I couldn't. It was too late because my kids needed rides or would be wondering about dinner. I would have seen him again, but after that, I never heard from him?!!? I was bummed, because I really thought he was my guy.

Until . . . a year later he messaged me that he would love to see me again, but then he went silent. Until . . . I texted him a few years later to ask what happened. He was truly the one that got away, and my curiosity caught up to me. He said he didn't think I liked him, and he really wanted to go out. We texted for a week and had plans to go out, but I never heard from him again. May he rest in peace. He didn't die; I just needed to put Wine Please to rest.

33. Virginia is for lovers

Virginia guy was hilarious. We texted and talked for hours. I found myself looking forward to our next interaction because he was so much fun. I laughed all day long in between raising teenagers and working.

Finally, we were going to meet at a whiskey bar in the city. I had sent him the address, but he went to the wrong place. This was one of the few times that I had to wait for a date. I understand the confusion because there are two places with the same name in the city. Well, he eventually showed up and was not attractive at all, and he was short. Still, I really liked him; he made me laugh. We had several cocktails, then dinner, then more cocktails, and I Ubered with him to his hotel room. We made out in the lobby for a while and then went to his room. We did not go all the way, but his skill level was intoxicating. Amazing. He begged me to have sex, but I declined and he took it well thankfully. He paid for me to take an Uber home. He was a very classy guy. It was a great time, and I looked forward to seeing him again. We were going to meet up the next morning, but he was ignoring my texts. I figured he was still asleep. He finally texted that something came up, and he had to get back to Virginia. He went silent for a while.

Eventually he texted me that I live too far away, and he couldn't afford hotels. Whatever, dude. Several months later, he messaged me to say that I was a nice girl. Weirdo. The takeaway from this is that I had to eliminate guys from Virginia because I couldn't drive that far. I started to realize that most guys just want sex, and a second date was never part of their plan.

34. Coach

Coaches fascinate me. I missed my calling. Being able to motivate a variety of personalities and bring them together as a team is an art. Coach was an awesome first date. He was an amazing kisser. He had lived a very interesting life. Mom basically left him alone to raise himself. Good looking, tall. Great words and texts. Did I mention *greaaaaattttt* kisser? He sent me photos and articles and kept in touch in a very welcomed way. He made me smile, and I thought he really liked me.

We went on four dates, and each was more fun than the last. I was even planning on coming to one of his games. We had a connection. After date five, I went to his place and had amazing sex. He was skilled and could maneuver well; he had been an athlete after all. Afterward he fell asleep. I mean dead asleep. I decided to take an Uber home because I didn't want to wake him up and I had to go home. I left a cute note on a napkin.

The next day he started texting me at 6 am.

"Where did you go??"

"Why did you leave!!?"

I replied, "I left a note." He was livid that I left. Keep in mind, I told him I could not sleep over at the beginning of the night. Still, he was freaked out for some reason. This changed the momentum. We went out one more time, but he was a complete jerk, complaining about the dinner bill which was only $80. At one point, he said lots of women *say* they are single moms, but they really aren't. Excuse me? Was he calling me a liar? He was also put off because I asked him to drive me home in his jalopy.

I did like him, for the record, and I pictured myself dating him for a while. On the way home, I said, "Look, I know you were mad about me Ubering home, but really, isn't that every man's dream?" He smiled at that because he knew I was right. But the momentum had changed, and I texted that I had to let him go.

A few years later, I saw him in the parking lot walking into a restaurant with a first date (I could tell from the awkward way they were walking and talking). I was walking my dog at the time. He didn't see me. Then a year after that, he actually messaged me on a dating app. He didn't remember me. I responded with something like, "How could you forget me? Am I the only one who Ubered home, which is every guy's dream except for yours?" He wrote back and *still* didn't remember me. This perfectly illustrates the difference between guys and girls. I spent hours talking about him, analyzing him, and thinking about him. Meanwhile he never gave me a second thought. I never wrote him back. It just wasn't meant to be.

35. Ex Part Deux

I have a friend who refused to date guys with the same name as her ex-husband. Which would have been hard if he was named Kevin, Michael, or John, but I have to agree with her. I never went out with a guy who had the same name as my ex. I can't even stand to *see* his name, let alone date someone with that name. I *did* go on a quick date with a man who didn't look like my ex, but his story was the same.

I met Ex Part Deux at a romantic spot. I didn't drink because as usual, I had to pick up my kid. He was attractive enough and seemed very upbeat. As his story unfolded, it started to sound eerily familiar. The thrill was gone between him and his wife. Once again, he thought that the initial infatuation phase was going to last forever. He loved her, but wasn't *in love* with her. So, he had an affair, then left his wife and kids to move to a farm with his now second ex-wife.

I give him credit for telling the truth. I guess the similarities didn't really hit me at first because we were having fun. I was actually considering a second date. Once I replayed the tape of our date in my mind, I realized that this guy was my ex Part Deux! I knew it would have been impossible to get over the knowledge that he too left his wife and kids for a new life. Incidentally, my friend who wouldn't date guys with her ex's name met a great guy on a dating app.

She went out with him at the spur of the moment because another guy stood her up that day. They met later that evening, had instant chemistry, were on the same page about life goals and were married soon after, which was exceedingly brave of her. She married him about a month later. I am happy to report that five years later, they are still married and doing well.. You *can* find your happily ever after. Sometimes you may have to take a leap of faith, but it does exist.

36. Love Languages

It's so interesting that guys often reference *The Five Love Languages* written by Gary Chapman (1992) in their profiles. I wonder if they were introduced to the book during their last-ditch effort to save their marriage through couples counseling. The main takeaway from the book is that everyone has a preferred two out of five love languages.

The five are: words of affirmation, acts of service, receiving gifts, quality time, and physical touch. Guys inevitably claim that their number one love language is physical touch. I swear this is true for 99% of men. Translated this means sex. Is anyone surprised by this? Often the other love language tends to be quality time. Most guys want to spend time outdoors or play sports. Ideally they want to have sex in the outdoors while playing a sport. It is funny to me that they think they are revealing an innermost secret. We know guys, you want to have sex. It is the only reason they are dating in the first place.

About twelve years prior to his departure, I learned that my ex's love language was being hugged. He hated being touched, yet he really liked to be hugged. This surprised me, but from then on, I hugged him when he got home from work every day. I was happy to see him and would drop everything to embrace him. He was my favorite person. Hmmm, but even the love languages couldn't save our marriage from a tragic ending.

The love languages are worth exploring to at least discover something new about yourself as you are looking for a potential partner. Knowledge is power. Not knowing what you or they like or want is a disadvantage. I'm guessing that my brother-in-law's love languages would be words of affirmation and receiving gifts, so he would be an exception to this rule. He loves when you compliment his cooking and gets beyond excited when receiving gifts. He loves giving gifts too and is very generous. Sometimes what someone does is what they want done for them, and sometimes it is not. I've mostly seen physical touch in dating profiles though. Guys are easy to please. They are simple creatures, which really makes them lovable.

37. The Bowler

I've heard that some guys have a contest among friends to see who can spend the least amount of money on a girl before she puts out. I had been talking to a guy via text for a year. Yes, this goes against my rule of not texting for more than a week before meeting someone. I suggested places to go, and he didn't like the places. He refused to tell me his last name and that was a no-go for me.

He was very chatty, and he made me laugh, so I kept talking to him sporadically. I always end a conversation once my kids jump into my car, no matter who it is. The Bowler thought this was because I was married. He could not understand why I wouldn't talk to him while the kids were in the car. The answer is simple. First, I won't even talk to my sister, my besties, or my mom—nobody because this could be the only time I have to spend with the kid or kids all day, so I give them my full attention. Plus I didn't want them to hear that side of me. You know, kind of giddy.

I have made exceptions in emergency situations. My friend just had a grandchild, so I talked to her. Someone's husband lost a job; I can't just hang up in a crisis situation. Ninety-nine percent of the time I am focused on the kids. Often, kids don't want to talk, so we just crank up the music.

Driving is the easy part of parenting. Some days, I have made up to thirty trips. Guarantee that from the kids' point of view, I was *always* talking on the phone when they were in the car.

The Bowler had bowled professionally. He was a salt-of-the-earth guy. Great golfer too, liked to gamble, and didn't drink. He was a recovered addict.

I'm embarrassed to say that our "dates" consisted of me going to his house. I felt like I had known him for a long time, though, and I liked being there. Eventually, I did have sex with him. A week later, I was out with friends and was going to Uber to his house after. He didn't like that idea because one of them was a guy. We were just friends, but the Bowler insisted that I just hang out with him instead. Just hanging out at his house was getting old. I went out instead and had a fabulous time. The Bowler was furious that I went out. He wouldn't answer my texts. He called a week later, but by then I knew it was over. He sent a mean text about me still being married. Whatever, dude. Buh-bye. Was he playing that game? I wonder to this day. Newsflash! Guys are competitive, and they always like to win. I'm going with yes, he was playing the spend-nothing-and-get-laid game. He won, I lost. Or did I?

38. My Dream Man

I met my Dream Man one night at a going away party. He was a close friend of one of my cousins. I loved him before I met him based on how he treated my cousin. He was so caring and always checking in with my then unemployed cousin on speaker phone. I was so excited to finally meet him because part of me was already sold on him as a person. I was kind of surprised by how attractive he was. The three of us had planned to go out for happy hour, but my cousin was a no show. It ended up being just the two of us. Maybe my cousin really wasn't tied up at work after all. We shall never know the answer to that. In any case, he would have been the third wheel and he probably had much better things to do.

We had drinks at what later became our favorite local bar, then we went to another restaurant. I never wanted the night to end. My Dream Man had been a college athlete. He had an understated confidence that was so sexy. He was so funny, he always made me laugh every time we talked. He was maybe five ten, and his body was solid—thick and masculine. The kind of man who I knew could protect me in any situation, and while that's old-fashioned, it is hot. He had a sly smile and cute way about him that I was fiercely attracted to. One of the reasons I was attracted to him was that his BFF was the opposite of him, yet he adored him. One was conservative, the other liberal. One smoked pot, the other just drank. One had several kids, the other had none. One went to church, the other didn't. People were ending friendships over politics. These two BFFs were diabolically opposed, but they loved each other unconditionally. I respected that. I think that is rare for a man.

What I loved most was that Dream Man was an amazing father to his three kids. He chose them above everything else. He took them on trips individually. He went to all their games, tournaments, and hosted parties for prom photos. He was all about being a dad one hundred percent. This was so attractive to me because I meant for my kids to have a dad like that too. He was going through a separation at the time but was still living in his family home because he didn't want to be away from the kids. I had met a few guys who teetered on the edge of leaving but couldn't because of the kids. I admired that.

I proceeded with caution, since Dream Man still lived at home. Everyone knows that means they may never leave. After our first date he was all I could think about. Oh my goodness, talk about chemistry! We went on the most romantic and wholesome dates. A picnic, a sunset dinner, walks. Each date we only kissed, which was refreshing after being with many guys who just wanted to have sex with me and as many women as possible before they died.

But the anticipation was building. One night we went out with several other people, and I had a hotel for the night. We took it to the next level. It was magical and amazing. We dated on and off for many years. We talked and texted frequently as well. Sometimes about our kids, or our jobs, or about my cousin or other friends. Sometimes it was all about sex. It just depended on the day. One time I even slept over at his house. Now that was a slice of heaven, maybe too much. Then I wouldn't hear from him for a while and that was really challenging. I admit that when I was feeling especially close to him, I would date someone else—my way of protecting myself.

I had not seen Dream Man in six months, and I had resigned myself to not seeing him anymore. My cousin was in town and a bunch of us met up. Dream Man professed his undying love for me, and I rolled my eyes, but inside I was right back in. I saw him three times that week, and things were great. For a while. Then we repeated our pattern of being close then pulling away. I knew he could not leave his kids. Honestly, I did not want him to. I would never want to put someone through that. And the kids deserved to have their dad around a hundred percent of the time. I dated other people, but still saw him. On most of the other dates, I found myself wishing it had been Dream Man instead. I was in love but a kind of fake love. I knew it wasn't real. At least I was aware of that, but I was tormented by it at the same time. I respected him for staying, and I knew he would never leave. Maybe our connection was so electric because it wasn't real? We would never progress to the next level of comfort, boredom, monotony, and chores. I recognize that, I really do. I fantasize about him coming over with champagne and proposing after his last kid goes to college. In my heart of hearts, I know Dream Man will never leave. Alas, he will remain forever just a dream.

39. The Marine

At this point, you are shaking your head and thinking that I need some serious therapy. You're not wrong, but I'm starting to think I am just not the marrying kind. I tried it once and it didn't work out. Plus lots of the marrieds don't seem that happy. Variety is the spice of life, right?

In the fifteen years that I worked for the military, I dated extensively; however, I never dated a Marine. Trust me, I wanted to. The few, the proud? Yes, it's true, they are a rare band of hot brothers, and there is just something especially attractive about a Marine. My dad was a Marine, so I am sure Freud would say that explains it. I think because I never dated one that added to my intrigue. So finally, I got to date a Marine. COVID lockdown was in full swing, and people were dying left and right. My hundred kids were home from school on the e-learning grind. My son was blissfully sleeping or gaming while attending class. It was a dream come true for him. Not for me, though. I needed to get out of the house. And I did—on one of the best of my many dates.

He was a Marine. I would say former or retired, but that is frowned upon by the Marines. Once a Marine, always a Marine. His current career was sales at a high-end construction company. We met in the middle of the day at a wedding overlook place, and he brought two chairs and a cooler full of snacks and drinks. He had us situated six feet apart. It was so creative and so much fun.

After a few hours of chatting and laughing, I had to take a call. I had a strict policy against that because once I took a call from my kid in the middle of a date and he proceeded to ask me if we had any salsa. While I was on the call with an insurance company, he came over and kissed me. It was nice but what about being six feet apart? I totally lost my concentration. After that we went to the little farmers market inside the wedding place. He bought me organic eggs. It was so romantic. A few days later we went on a mini hike. I really liked him. I am not sure why, but he stopped texting. It's all good. I still love Marines: Semper Fi.

40. The Bird Watcher

The bird watcher was my first FaceTime call. My kids are much more comfortable on FaceTime than I am. Many of the guys I dated didn't even like to text, or know how. I reluctantly agreed to my one and only FaceTime call. I made sure the camera was above me and the lighting was dim. Fuzzy lighting is key. For the record, I don't even like to be on camera for work meetings, family Zoom, sorority Zoom. It is so distracting. I can't concentrate on what anyone is saying because I'm trying to make sure I look good. I can't get past myself.

The Bird Watcher seemed nice. He was a prior Air Force pilot and was divorced twice with a teenage daughter. He was not attractive at all, by anyone's standards. He invited me to go bird watching and I agreed. This is comical because he made me wear the little harness and everything. It was actually fun. He would interrupt the conversation to show me a bird. I really enjoyed it, although I was worried that someone would see me geeking out in a binocular harness. I asked for a ride from him, and he said he would if I kissed him. Horrible kisser but an overall fun time. We had another dreaded FaceTime call, and he sent me a video of him singing. I give him a lot of credit for sending it because it was comical. He could not sing at all. He asked me out again, then later canceled. Some BS about his daughter being immuno-compromised with COVID, and he couldn't take any chances. I only agreed to go out with him on the second date, because my sixteen year old daughter said I was too picky, and I needed a boyfriend. Still, I must say, the birding date was one of the most fun and memorable dates.

41. The Texters

Early on, you begin to realize that some guys do not want to meet, they just want to text. Although they never tell you that they have no intention of meeting up, they just string you along for days, weeks, years. I assume this is because they are married or involved or possibly catfishing for kicks. When Ohio BFF took over managing my dating life, we both fell in love with a guy named Matt. Let me clarify, she thought he was the perfect match for me. Matt was tall and exceedingly good looking. He was a surfer. A Stanford educated attorney. He was who she imagined that I would end up with. I believe she is still holding out hope for Matt and I, seven years later.

There came a point when the three of us were texting and eventually she backed out. I talked to and texted Matt for years. He was smart and we had great conversations. We made plans to meet many times, but eventually I realized it was never going to happen. Now we text once a year, or less, and he offers to meet up. I agree, fully knowing that we never will and questioning the validity of his identity.

A lot of these guys are not scammers, they just want a texting relationship. One texter was hilarious and we chatted many times. I really loved talking to him. He called me gran, which was hysterical. He was twelve years younger than me.

For some reason, I loved that nickname. We made plans to meet a few times, but he cancelled every time, so I had to block him. I don't like the feeling of getting connected to someone who may not have ill intentions but is never going to meet me. Generally, I will only text someone for a week and then if he doesn't ask me on a date I'm out. I thought maybe this texting phenomenon was exclusive to the elderly, but my cousin's daughter told me that a lot of her guy friends in their mid-twenties prefer texting to actually going out. They say it's a lot easier—less drama, cheaper, and less complicated. I have a colleague who texted and talked to her now husband for hours and weeks prior to meeting because of COVID and work schedules. They fell in love over the phone, then began dating, got engaged and are happily married. In her case, she had already known him when they were both married to other people. So, I should clarify that if it's a stranger and you have been texting and talking but he doesn't ask you out, buyer beware. Texting can be deceiving.

42. Feels like the first time

It was my first time going out to a restaurant since being sequestered by COVID. We met up at an outdoor restaurant right near my house. Being out again was exhilarating. It was perfect weather, and I was so excited just to be there. He was a small, very cute guy. We had so much fun; the date lasted three and half hours. The whole time I was with him I knew I'd never go out with him again, but I thoroughly enjoyed the time together. Several red flags were popping up during the date. First of all, he wasn't divorced yet. Second, he talked about how much he hated his wife. Third, money seemed to be a significant problem. For instance, he didn't have insurance for five years. I mention this date because it was a lot of fun. Not all first dates lead to a second date, but you can still really enjoy someone's company. He was great, just not right for me.

43. Tall, Dark, and Handsome

This guy was hot, I mean, perfection in a man. He had lats for days, tanned skin, a perfect smile, and was six four. He was a former pro athlete, legitimately. Obviously I fact checked it. He had been married twice and was raising his younger two kids by himself. He had just started his own business prior to COVID, so the timing wasn't great. His mom helped him with the kids when he had to travel. We went for a walk and hung out several times. He was low on funds, so we never really went on a proper date, but he was intriguing and definitely some major eye candy. Maybe he and the Bowler were playing that game where you see how little you can spend on a girl before she puts out?

Tall, dark, and handsome was a man of few words, but sometimes he said some very insightful things. Once he told me that I should stop trying to get my ex to see the kids because all he could offer is fake love, and they deserve real love. He was right. He also wore a rubber band around his wrist. He used to wear hair ties on his wrist because his daughter always needed one. Once she grew up, he no longer needed to carry them, but he replaced the hair tie with a brown rubber band. He would occasionally pluck the rubber band to remind himself of the important things in life. I admired him. Was it him or his intoxicating looks?

At times he had almost a bitter disposition. I couldn't figure out if he didn't want to be seen with me or if he truly didn't have enough money to take me out. We talked and texted, and sometimes I went to his house. One Saturday night, I was driving over at midnight to pick up Taco Bell for him. Of course at his request. I told my kids I was going to his house and would be home in an hour. One screamed, "a booty call?!!" Ugg BUSTED, except I wasn't having sex with him. Tall, Dark and Handsome may have been a skilled athlete, but he was challenged in the bedroom. Probably from having copious amounts of sex during his pro athlete days. My teenagers did make me realize that I was ridiculous. A 50 something woman going over to a guy's house at midnight to make out? But he was sooo attractive. Sadly, I said goodbye to Tall, Dark, and Handsome.

44. A Normal Dad

Now, this guy was such a nice, wholesome dad. He was in sports marketing, and we had a great time talking about local teams and players. He had two sons who lived with him part of the time. They went to a private school. I wondered if my daughters knew them because they have thousands of followers. He divorced his wife because she was boring and never wanted to have sex. A common theme among the fifty-something wives, or at least their ex-husbands' view of them.

He was so cute, not tall, and balding, but had a certain charisma. I really liked him. Like all my preferred men, he made me laugh. His Bumble profile mentioned that he had a special skill. I was intrigued. Turns out when he and his wife were first married, they went to a tantric sex seminar. It reminded me of that *Sex and the City* episode where Charlotte drags her friends to the seminar that takes place in an elderly couple's home. They are watching the woman perform and giggling the whole time, then Charlotte gets squirted on. Hilarious.

The couples in Normal Dad's seminar would learn various techniques then go back to their rooms to try them out. He claims that he learned to make women have the most amazing orgasms of their lives. Say what? Really now, I wondered if this was true? Most women cannot orgasm with penetration alone. This is a well-known fact among women, but men didn't get the memo for some reason. Of course, I was curious about this special skill, and I really like him, so I went on a second date. That was when I learned that he had an affair when he was married, but they caught feelings and had to break it off. After that, he went on a dating app for married people to hook up with like-minded marrieds. He told a crazy story about a woman meeting up with him who had very specific criteria. He had to wear black, he had to tie her up, etc. Then he told me that he frequented swinger and sex clubs. There was nothing normal about this dad. No judgment at all but that is not for me. He was looking for wild group sex and he needed a plus one. I guess I should have read between the lines. Turns out that Normal Dad was an insatiable sex addict. Thanks, but no thanks.

45. Timing

Timing really is everything when it comes to late-in-life relationships. Congrats if it has worked out for you in your fifties because the stars must align for both parties at the same time. When you're young, the hope is still alive that you will fall in love and run off into the sunset and live happily ever after. Young people are generally on the same page. Fast forward to age fifty something. The pages are ripped and out of order and missing.

A person with young kids is not going to mesh with someone who has college-aged kids. One person might be retired, while the other is tied down to a job. One person wants to move to the beach, the other to the city. It's a miracle the timing is right for so many couples. Most people I dated had grown kids. The majority of guys were not looking for the second or third Mrs. Right. Guys, generally speaking, want freedom. If someone has just been relieved of their marital obligation, they may go into what is known as the "ho phase" and hook up with everything that's not nailed down. It's exciting to do anything and anybody you want. Others have no interest in the "ho phase," or have been there and have moved on, looking for a relationship. Maybe there is truly never a good time to try to commit again, but so many people do, it is amazing. The odds are that timing is going to work for you if you work for it.

46. Oh, no!

He was a family acquaintance. He was great looking, Latin, married with one child. We had not seen him in years, but my family had noticed that he started to look really tired and sometimes even doze off. People are tired, though, and we brushed it off. About four years since any of us had seen him, he started posting memes that made it obvious that his wife had left him.

I reached out via messenger, and he contacted me to go for drinks. It wasn't necessarily a date-date, but I was looking forward to seeing him and hearing his story. We hugged, he was really skinny where once he had been thicker. He wanted to know how I knew his wife left him. He asked me several times. I guess it was the language barrier, but he was posting things like: *It hurts the most when you still love them, but they are gone.* Ummm . . . pretty sure that would explain it, but he was sure someone had told me. He couldn't imagine how I knew. He immediately started ordering double mojitos. He explained that he had been addicted to Xanax, and he went to detox but refused to go to rehab, so his wife left him. He was telling me this while ordering drink after drink.

Then he started showing me photos of his twenty-some-thing girlfriends. Okay . . . it's definitely **not** a date. Then he asked me out of the blue if I liked him, if I want to date him. Instead of saying "Hell, no!", you're clearly an addict, I gingerly explained that I really didn't have time to date being the sole parent. I felt for him, he clearly missed his wife because he talked about her the entire date. This was the one and only time I texted my sister from the bathroom, gave him an excuse that one of the kids needed a ride, then left money on the table, and ran out of there. He texted me later to say he wanted to show me his place and was sorry I had to leave. I couldn't get mixed up in that storm of addiction, ho phase, and missing his wife. Years later, we learned through Facebook that he met a woman and moved to another state to be with her. Best wishes to them.

47. What was I thinking?

There is only one date that I truly regret. Here's what happened. We met up in the parking lot and hugged as usual. He was tall and great looking. He said that I was his first date, and he was going through a divorce. He also had a lot of kids but the youngest was a freshman in college. His wife didn't want to have sex anymore and he wanted out. Same ol' same ol'. There was hella great chemistry. It was magnetic. He was interesting and honest. He wanted to know about me and acted empathic and impressed that I was a single mom with a full-time job.

Here's where I may have made a crucial error. I agreed to do a tequila shot. I am not sure why, but he was very persuasive and I instantly liked him a lot. I just had one, though, so it really doesn't explain everything. We connected on every topic. He was in sales so I should have known that I was being sold a dream. He was saying all the right things, doing all the right things. I texted my sister and Ohio BFF that he was the one—I have finally found my man. I had no intention of getting married but I really wanted a boyfriend.

We were making plans to see each other again. He seemed genuine. I feel like an idiot now, but I went to his place. We knew some of the same people, so I felt safe. And yes, we did it. I am **not** that girl, and I can't to this day really explain why or how I went from zero to one thousand, but I did. As he was driving me back to my car, he said, "I don't regret what happened at all." An odd statement. I was confused because I was sure we would see each other again. The next day, I texted him to see if he wanted to get together, and he couldn't but promised to reach out ASAP. I didn't hear from him until weeks later, and he said I owed him a date. By then, I realized I had been duped and that he was just looking for a fling. I still think about why I did that. I was not drunk at all. It was so unlike me. Was there something in my drink? I guess it was just bad judgment and wishful thinking.

48. Divorce?

What is the allure of divorce? Why do some people avoid it like the plague while others seem to gravitate toward it? Is it because divorce offers another chance at the illusion or delusion of happiness? Is hot sex a euphemism for happiness? Is divorce an excuse to relive the days when you didn't have responsibility? Your relationship was a clean slate. Feelings had not been hurt. Expectations were intact. Do the divorced want to get that back? When I was single in my early thirties, I had a financial advisor who was roughly my age at the time. He gave me unsolicited advice, as lots of people will. He said, "Never marry someone who is divorced because it is part of their vocabulary." I had heard this before from a cheating hot mess of a friend: "If you don't want to do something, don't do it once."

I have some friends who think everyone is divorced. Most people go through life as part of a couple. A friend is going through a divorce which her husband initiated. Several of his divorced guy friends told him that the only advice they have for him is to not get divorced. I have several friends who regret getting divorced as well. I'm not sure you can prepare for the anguish you undergo. My sorority sisters told me that after the first year, I'd be glad to be divorced. Five years have passed, and I've never been glad to be divorced. My life is not better nor easier. The heartbreak lives within me like the shingles virus. I'd like to say it was the best thing that ever happened to me. I'd like to say my kids are better off. I'd like to say I didn't realize how great my life would be with someone else. I can't because I'm not a liar. On the other hand, I have cousins who married young, then went on to remarry, and the second time was better. Most of the guys I dated were divorced once, sometimes twice. I can honestly say that most of the guys I met were happy with their decision to divorce. Guys are better at brushing themselves off and getting back up again after the fall. I think some people have unrealistic expectations of marriage. People think the excitement of the first year is going to last forever, and it doesn't. It can't. Life takes over and an enduring, loving relationship sets in. I once tried to explain this to my single brother. He thought this happened to me but wouldn't happen to him and his then fiancée. Trying to explain this phenomenon is like explaining what seeing is to a blind person. Seeing is believing or rather if you've been married, you know.

49. Secret Service

I met this guy for less than an hour. He was kind of mysterious. I guess because he had worked for the Secret Service.
I sometimes wonder how many guys are married and still
meeting up with girls all over the place. How hard would it
be to travel for your job and just go out on dates? He gave
me this vibe. Secret Service wasn't my favorite to text with or
talk to. He was very serious, but asked lots of sex related questions. When we met, he talked about his colleagues who were
all divorced. One guy had just married a lady, and he was
her sixth husband!? Really? Number six is the charm? I don't
understand her or the guys who married her. She did have
ginormous implants, so maybe that was the attraction? Secret
Service talked a lot about how all his friends' wives had fake
boobs and they got divorced anyway, so who really knows?

Here's the interesting thing about Secret Service. He
loved his wife, and they had great sex. Out of the near 100
guys I dated, this was the only time I heard that from a guy. I
told him that he should have stayed with her. Again with the
unsolicited advice . . . sometimes I can't help myself. He said
that he liked to mountain bike, and she liked to knit, that's
why he left her. What?? What guy in his right mind cares
about hobbies when the sex is great? Go mountain biking

with your sixth husband friend. He's going to need a break from Dolly. Secret Service lived with a woman for five years and then another for six months.

We only met once. He asked if I wanted to go out again and I said sure, but I wasn't really motivated. He contacted me again six months later via a dating app and had forgotten we went out. He asked for a full-length photo. I said nah— you already saw me in person! Maybe Secret Service was one of the guys hooking up while he was still married.

50. So Great, and Then Not

This was my guy! We talked and texted for weeks. We talked for more than twenty hours over a week. It was wonderful and sometimes he would call for 30 seconds, just to tell me something. There was a COVID scare that delayed our date. Finally, we met in person at an outdoor venue on the water. I went up to him. He turned around and he was clearly disappointed. It was upsetting. He was completely different and unenthusiastic. We left that place because the wait was too long, and he was very irritated. It wasn't going well.

Where was my funny, giddy, talkative man? He didn't touch me, never complimented me, never acted happy to see me. The fatal flaw: He was borderline rude to the wait staff. How could this guy who I liked so much be so different in person? Maybe this was a temporary glitch? We had a mutual colleague in common, so it felt safe to go to his house after our date. Have you seen *Sleeping with the Enemy*, a nineties movie about a guy who is over-the-top OCD. That was his house and pantry. His nephew would purposely move his canned goods just to bother him. My family and friends are reading this thinking, "Now, that is the pot calling the kettle black!" I'm here to tell you that he makes me look like a slob, and he doesn't have kids or a dog so his level of perfection could not be matched. Yes we kissed but there was nothing there. He drove me home and was complaining about how far away my house was. I didn't hear from him for a few days after that. He had been texting me twenty times a day. I had to let him go. He wasn't my guy. I guess he was hoping I'd look like his former fiancée. She was a tiny twenty-five-year-old beauty. No comparison, I can't compete with that. She cheated on him, by the way.

51. Dutch?

Some women would not think of letting a man pay for her drinks, dinner, coffee, or anything. Many insist on paying for themselves. They do not want to feel like they owe the guy a hug or kiss, or anything further. They want to keep the relationship on even ground from the start. Some women will let the guy pay for the second date but never the first. That way she can walk away without any guilt.

Here is where I differ. I was raised in a generation where people went on dates and the gentlemen paid. Once when I was twenty-four, I went out with a guy in my sailing class who I was not attracted to at all. We actually called him Ugly Man. Yes, it was mean. He was nice, and honestly, I really didn't know how to say no to him because he asked me out while we were in mid-jibe. I was contemplating getting together with a Navy Lieutenant who had a crush on me, but I was scared to pull the trigger on that relationship. Ugly Man was an engineer, owned his home, and had two cars. He made big boy money (as one of my BFF's daughters puts it). He insisted on meeting at, of all places, Red Lobster. When the check came, he pulled out coupons. At the time, I was horrified, but now I get it. Then he told me down to the penny how much I owed. I was dirt poor at the time, living paycheck to paycheck. I probably made $17,000 a year. After taxes that is about $900 a month. I had just taken my *last* $20 out of the ATM. He then asked me if I wanted to go to the movies, but I told him that I had run out of money. That date made me realize that I needed to pursue the Navy Lieutenant. I went to see him after the Red Lobster Debacle of 1989 and began one of the best relationships of my life. So, thank you, Ugly Man, for making me realize who I really wanted to be with. I would gladly be with the Navy Lieutenant to this day if that were an option.

To pay or not to pay? I only mention this story from my younger days because it shaped the way I think about paying for dates. After my divorce, I was terrified that I would be unable to keep it together financially. I had to make sure that I could pay the bills and any unexpected expenses that came along while having so many teens. The list goes on: braces, glasses, contacts, therapy, psychiatry, camps, sports, PT, medical bills, wisdom teeth extraction, clothes, shoes. It never ends. I drive a twelve-year-old car with 185,000 miles, and my kids share a twenty-year-old car with 250,000 miles. Some of these guys showed up driving $150,000 cars. Most of the men with a few exceptions could easily afford the dates we went on.

It has been my impression that most men my age or older want to pay for dates. I did not feel guilty. I did not feel like I owed them anything. I imagine that trying to split the check sends a business-like message and makes it awkward. I was extremely grateful that they paid. Twice, guys asked me to pay half. I was offended. Both were sixty-six years old, and both wanted to go out again. One of them owned three homes. Our bill was $52! Every teenage boy I know pays for dates, so yes, it bothered me. To the men, I suggest that if you plan on going Dutch, text your intentions before the date so that the woman does not misread splitting the check as a sign of disinterest. For the record I did pay for several third or fourth dates. Some guys still wouldn't let me, but I had my ways of paying anyway. Gutter minds? No, not the sexual ways, just sneaking the credit card before he had time to pay.

52. Tennis, anyone?

He was a very attractive guy who was a really great tennis player. His wife was mad at him because of a financial lie. By mad, I mean wouldn't sleep with him nor hug him and barely spoke to him for over a year. Wow, talk about a grudge! Of course, this is only one side of the story, but I find it very interesting. We met to play tennis. I played in high school but am terrible now. I recognized that our tennis time was charitable on his end. Immediately I wanted to be friends because I absolutely loved playing tennis with him. I wasn't interested in dating him for several reasons. One, I had a better track record being long-term friends with a guy rather than dating. That seems to be the kiss of death. Two, he seemed to want to get back together with his wife. Three, he wanted to move south in the near future. Finally, he lived in one of those co-op situations with three twenty-something girls. That seemed like a recipe for disaster, meaning he was bound to hook up or fall in love with one of them. Guys are age blind. We went out three times, and I really liked him; it was as if he was my tennis instructor. He texted me one day that he had met someone, and he couldn't see me anymore. I was happy for him but sad for me. I contemplated arguing that we were just friends. I mean, we had never even kissed after all! I decided against it. About six months later, I invited them to a bar with a bunch of my friends and my brother-in-law. Tennis told me he would come but he had broken up with his girlfriend. I was excited to see him. Dream Man was there in the beginning of the night but had to leave so the coast was clear. He showed up alone, told me he loved my hair curly, but the bar was too crowded for him, and he feared getting COVID. He left and I never heard from him again. In retrospect, maybe I should have gone outside with him to chat? Whateves, it's too late now. I do miss the tennis though.

53. Cancer

I dated four guys who had cancer, two who had had it in their late teens, but had been in remission for over thirty years. I really think one had a relapse, but he didn't know it yet.

Cancer had just been diagnosed, and while it was supposed to be nothing, it kept recurring. Cancer was not tall, but he was cute and so happy. We met for dinner in 2020, and he seemed giddy over me. Very affectionate and very fun in general. He and his wife were in the pharmaceutical sales careers. She cheated with a doctor, but he didn't seem too upset over it. Time heals all wounds, perhaps? He played golf every Friday with a group of guys who laughed, teased each other, and drank. Sounds like so much fun; he loved those guys. He was very mushy on texts: "I miss you." While some girls may steer away from that, I kind of liked it. It was refreshing. We went out again in 2021, and in between, he kept asking me out, but then had to cancel. In 2022, he had to undergo some more chemo and was in the hospital for a while. He bought a boat and wanted to go out, but we never did.

We have a mutual friend, and one day she asked me to lunch. I was worried that she was going to tell me he passed away. Instead, she told me that she didn't think I should date him. Oh my gosh, why? Was he married, a child molester?

No, none of those things, she just said he was a bit odd. I asked her in what way, and she said he would obsess over things. I never really understood what she was trying to say. I know that married people romanticize being single and long to be sometimes. They think that there are guys lined up and waiting to sweep you off your feet and run off into the sunset. At this age, the issues list is long. In our twenties, there were no issues. I had friends back then who wouldn't date a guy based on the kind of shoes they wore. Just finding someone with common interests, goals who you are also attracted to, is very challenging. At least it is for me. Marrieds just don't understand. I didn't go out with him again not because of her feedback, but we just kind of lost touch. He was great though.

54. Mustache Man

My sister says dating is closely linked to guys' love of the re-
mote control. They don't want to watch what's on, they want
to know what *else* is on. That can be dangerous. I heard once
in a movie that a girl didn't get married because she didn't
think the last guy who proposed would be the very last chance
for marriage Maybe that's why I decided to get married. Running out of options scared me.

Enter Mustache Man. We went on a date. He was tall,
good-looking, and happy. In the middle of a sentence, he
stopped to tell me that I looked really great. This was so kind
because after a while, when so many guys complained about
people not looking like their photos, you wonder if they think
you do. He had two sons, and his wife was a highly successful
businesswoman in the town where they lived. She was pretty
(yes I looked her up, never a good idea) and apparently nice
to everyone except him. I actually canceled another guy to go
out with Mustache Man the next night. He picked me up in
his sporty Jeep. The house was empty at the time. We were
sitting on the couch trying to decide where to go. We kissed
but nothing major. My son walked in and didn't notice us at
first until I said, "Hey, there," then introduced them. And
yes, it was awkward, but I'm sure my son didn't care at all. I

was shaken by it, but we still went on to have a fabulous time. Drinks, kisses, laughter. The next week I asked him if I could bring him dinner and he said, "I would have loved to, but I have my kids tonight and tomorrow night." Then, a few days later, he asked me to come over and I couldn't. This played out another time or two, then we lost touch. I decided to call him a few years later, and he was sweet, but he had moved to Virginia with his girlfriend. Definitely a missed opportunity. Hopefully this wouldn't be the last!

55. Nebraska

There are some states that I love. I trust and immediately like everyone from that state. Makes no sense, but it's how I roll. I once dated a Special Forces guy who originally hailed from Nebraska. He was such a good person, so that formed my opinion about the state. It proved me right because everyone else I have met from Nebraska has been kind.

I met Nebraska for a drink while my child was at practice. He was a manly man, very cute, and drove a truck, of course. I like that. He moved here for his son who had fifty-fifty custody of his four-year-old daughter. He loved his granddaughter and wanted to be closer to her and help his son. He stepped down from his high-level executive job to take a lesser job with the same company. Nebraska was kind but not easy to talk to. It wasn't like pulling teeth, but it wasn't easy either. Still, I would have gone out with him again. At the end of the date, he said, "Let's go out again." He told me that I should let him know when my child had practice again, and we could meet. I had mentioned several times that she had practice every day. I wasn't sure if he wanted to see me again or was just being nice. Several months later, he texted me a Valentine's Day message. I suggested that we go out again, but I never heard from him. I tried to find his number a year later, but I must have deleted it.

56. Being Stood Up

Yes, it happens. I got stood up. It happened to me for the first time and only time, seven years into my cereal dating career. I started chatting with a younger guy, aged fifty. Gary seemed real and although we hadn't talked much via the dating app, he wanted to meet. He said he would be in my area the following day and could we meet at 4:30. I suggested the place, and Gary said he loved that place. I arrived early and sat in my car watching discreetly at the people going inside. Although I hadn't seen him, I decided to go in and get a table near the bar. I messaged him on the app. He did not respond. I contemplated waiting thirty minutes but started walking out at the fifteen-minute mark and left after twenty minutes. I did not hear from Gary until nine a.m. the next morning. He said that he was there and looked everywhere for me. I blocked him. If this had been my first or second on-line date, I may have thrown in the towel but with experience comes wisdom. Gary was probably a group of teenage boys getting a kick out of messaging unsuspecting women. Or maybe he was real. Either way, I happily brought home carryout for my kids and never thought of Gary again.

57. Hunter-Fisher

Hunter-Fisher was a talker. This can be a lot of fun because it's almost like watching a movie. I was sick of my own stories and still didn't like to talk about my kids, so I rather enjoyed hearing about other people's divorces and their kid struggles or triumphs. We met at a place known for their crabcakes. Hunter-Fisher had not had a drink in thirty-three years. I greatly admire this, and it takes a lot of the issues out of a relationship. Add a lot of alcohol, and problems are sure to follow. His wife was an alcoholic, and she would not stop drinking no matter how much he pleaded with her. It is challenging when there are two drastically different levels of alcohol consumption within one couple. He told me lots of fishing and hunting stories that involved him and his best friend. The stories were very detailed, and I had a hard time keeping up with the particulars, but they were fun and held my interest. His adult son lived with him. He was a great kisser and like many before and after him, acted like he was very into me. He said he really wanted to see me again. We made plans several times to get together but alas, they never materialized, and I never saw him again.

58. Men

My favorite thing about men is their sex drive. Second to that it's hands down the pickup basketball game. Just shooting hoops with a bunch of strangers. It is just something girls don't do, and it's a shame because it looks like fun. I love to see a group of guys mountain biking, who are covered in dirt and happy as can be. Guys are full of testosterone, and they inherently like to move, hike, run, play sports, and just be outdoors.

My mom was a tomboy, and she embodied a lot of these traits. I love how when it comes to business, men don't hold a grudge or cry at work. When I entered the workforce, I would watch as guys yelled at one another, full-on screaming and slewing insults, and then civilly go out for beers or go for a run together. They could just let it go, not take it personally, and move on. I tried to be like that at work because I admire it. It's a great way to be and probably adds years to your life. My dad used to yell at me, and I would fight back tears, then run swiftly up to my room and bawl my eyes out. Don't get me wrong—women have some wonderful characteristics, too. They are compassionate and loving, good listeners, and they understand emotions. I hear a lot of my married friends complain about how their husbands don't listen or weren't compassionate enough when their mom died or when they had cancer. Yes, the reason is because you married a man. Empathy and compassion is what your girlfriends are for. Guys know how to play pickup basketball with strangers, but they often struggle with understanding emotions.

59. Packing

You know someone is young when they have a name like Lane. This guy was in his early forties. Might as well, right? The guys aspire to date someone twenty years younger so why not fourteen years younger? Of course, my suspicious nature and watching too many *Dateline* episodes had me wondering why a young guy would want to date an older woman with kids. Unless we are talking about a sugar mama, which clearly I am not.

We are not as much fun as a young thirty-five-year-old without kids. I'm speaking for myself, I guess, but we are tired, for one, and we are driving kids around 24/7. Our time is so limited, then there's the laundry—it never ends. Did I mention that we are tired? Who am I to argue though, the man wanted to date me, so I put my fears of being murdered aside and obliged. He had a way with texting that just can't be found in older guys. There's a comfort level with flirting that might have turned some girls off, but I found it refreshing and a little addictive. There are a lot of rules with texting and calling. *Don't text back right away. Don't talk too much. Don't be too available. Match their energy.* All created so you don't seem too eager or desperate.

This guy made me feel wanted. He made me feel sexy. He lived forty minutes away, which is really a deal breaker, but I met him anyway. He was a former military guy and an instructor of sorts at a nearby military base. He was packing, which was kind of hot. If he did turn out to be a hit man and used the gun on me, that would be a downer for sure. There's something hot about a man who wields a gun. I guess it's a hero/rescue type fantasy born long ago.

It was a chilly, dark November evening. We hugged in the parking lot. I know it's my thing, but I really don't like walking into a place and looking for my date. Walking in together makes it seem like we know each other. It's less awkward. Of course, we met at a bar. Do guys want to sit at the bar so they can limit the date to one drink then leave? He was very interesting. I love the military, so hearing about his job was exciting to me. His dad had been a high-ranking officer and although he graduated from college, he enlisted instead of going the officer route, to his dad's dismay. He also told stories about his twin brother. At the end of the date, we kissed. I was into him. He asked me to come to his condo. I declined. He texted me after and then ghosted me. I was surprised because he was very lovey-dovey, baby this-and-that in his texts. I guess he had just wanted to hook up, or murder me, we shall never know.

60. Deprise

My sister and I made up a word to describe the letdown that occurs when you are anticipating something really wonderful only to be disappointed. Expectations and fantasies can be fun while they last, but the aftershock of reality can be so disappointing. It's like that Christmas gift someone is so excited to give you, and you have to feign excitement after opening it. Sometimes her husband would tell her that he had a surprise for her and then reveal that he was taking her and the kids to a hotel. Now this may have been fun for him, but moms of babies know that any trip or outing is a vacation for the kids but often very difficult for the mom. Just packing the diapers and supplies for a hotel stay can take hours. Then if you forget the wipes, that involves a trip to the store. Don't get me started on sleep because throwing kids into a new environment can wreak havoc on their sleep, resulting in no sleep for the mom while the dad just slumbers away.

My generous brother-in-law's heart was in the right place as it always is, but the surprise was actually a *deprise* for my sister. I think dating and relationships can suffer from the deprise as well. Most women go through the pain, agony, and fun of dating so that someday they can meet someone to sail off into the sunset with. I wonder, though, is it really a prize? Marriage? Long-term relationships? Look around at the marrieds you know. Are they truly happy? Are they having great sex if they are even having sex at all? I just wonder if the end goal is really a prize or is it a deprise? One reason I am not too keen on the never-marrieds is because they do not have a realistic view of marriage. My close friend met her husband in tenth grade. Together for nearly forty years! She is an executive, and I asked her if she ever thought about having sex with someone else. She told me that she has never met a man, executive, dad, or stranger who she wanted to sleep with. Never! I would call BS on her, but she's honest, and she would tell me. That same friend once gave me the best marriage advice I've ever received. Let your commitment sustain your love. She said that sometimes she wakes up and her husband is sound asleep and breathing peacefully. He hasn't done anything wrong. For no reason at all, she is irritated at him. This was an eye-opening revelation for me. I had no idea people felt this way. They were best friends, committed, lifelong partners, all of their memories are intertwined. How is this possible? After I was married, I understood. I have to say, though, that I rarely felt that way about my ex, but we were only together eighteen years. He was easy to live with. We never fought. I was happy to see him every day. Very ironic, I was the proverbial, last to know.

Getting back to the deprise: Sometimes I wonder if I finally meet someone, the one I've been searching for, will it be a deprise? Is cereal the best part of dating? Would I be bored with one guy? Probably.

61. Burning Man

My Arizona BFF came for a visit. She's originally from Texas and is just a bottle of sunshine, so we love having her visit. My kids, my mom, my sister . . . We all adore her. She has been happily married for thirty-five years. Her husband is a joy. We used to take trips to Mexico and the Dominican Republic when I was married, and I miss that so much.

This was the first time AZ BFF had visited since my divorce. We went out to my favorite bar for my sister's birthday, but it was a deprise for her because my friend and I got rather tipsy and my sister was the designated driver. I have tried to make it up to her since because I highly doubt that is how she wanted to spend her birthday. At the bar, I was texting Dream Man from my sister's phone while my BFF was perusing dating profiles on my phone. She was talking about each guy as if she was shopping for a new house, reading off the attributes but mostly just deleting them immediately and laughing or making a disgusted face. "Ohhh, he's cute, six one, lives in Virginia." My sister chimed in: "Delete!" BFF was shocked, then understood that it's too far away.

This played out maybe forty times. The handsome thirty-year-old bartender was laughing at us. We asked if he's on the apps, and he told us the story of his engagement. Ah, young love, so sweet. Eventually, BFF continued messaging guys. I didn't care because it doesn't matter. I just let her message away. We told her a guy was fake, and she mistakenly sent "you're a fake" to the wrong guy. It was just a comedy of errors.

Finally, she came upon a guy who was going through a divorce. Normally I would not seek out this situation, but after a few drinks and texting my Dream Man, I didn't care. She explained that she was visiting from Arizona, and he offered to take both of us out. At the time, this was a first for me, but I was game. Later that night, I couldn't help but lecture the bartender about not leaving his kids when his marriage gets difficult. "No matter what," I implored, "please don't leave your kids." The poor guy was trying to close up, but he promised me that he wouldn't. As if anyone ever would—the thought is preposterous. My sister was just shaking her head at the whole scene and probably wondering what she did to deserve such a birthday deprise.

Two days later, AZ BFF and I ventured out to the Four Seasons lower lounge. It is a lovely and classy well-appointed living room–style lounge area. I warned her that most dates are not this high class and not to get her hopes up. Maybe the pep talk was for me. He was already there sitting in a comfortable chair as the December sunlight streamed in through the sheer curtains. He was sipping wine and got up to greet us. He was wearing a sport coat and khakis. He was short and channeling somewhat of a cute leprechaun look. He reminded me of one of the loves of my life. We gracefully took our seats, then ordered guacamole with pomegranate seeds and seltzer water.

He did most of the talking, which was fine with me. He had the confidence of a CEO and the compassion of a psychologist. He began regaling us with stories of business deals in Asia. We learned about his brother who had recently passed away and his children. He was the kind of storyteller that made you hang on his every word. He had been to Burning Man, an annual, nine-day gathering in the Nevada desert. It's held the week prior to and including Labor Day weekend each year and includes artistic performances, installations, music, and a lot of partying and experimenting. It culminates in the burning of a giant wooden statue. That was when the guy found himself and decided to leave his wife of fifteen years. This kind of struck a nerve because my ex had been living it up at Burning Man while I was home saddled with raising a bunch of wounded teenagers. I was able to push that aside and focus on our date. The most endearing thing about him was his compassion for my situation. He seemed to listen intently when we spoke and would ask a thoughtful question as a follow-up. He made quite an impression on us. While I waited for my car, we hugged and kissed after he took a call from one of his kids. We had plans to go out again, and lo and behold, it just never seemed to work out. Due to COVID, he wanted to sit outside in twenty-degree weather, and there really weren't options to do so. He suggested going to a hotel to have a picnic, which I would have readily done later on in a relationship, but not for a second date. We never had that second date.

62. You Never Know

Christmas was approaching. So much to do, and so little time. Still, I made time to comb through dating profiles, chuckling at the things guys wrote. "I'm seeking a LTR (long term relationship) with a woman whose true beauty lies within." Uhhh . . . delete. Liar. After several more deletes, I matched with a guy. I had long ago stopped checking guys out to see if we had mutual friends. I was at the point in the quest where I thought the less pre-texting the better. Sometimes you knew so much about someone that once you meet in person, there was nothing left to say. We never spoke, just decided to meet at a bar near a store I had to go to about an hour from my house. He was great-looking, tall, and happy. We sat at the bar and played trivia, which was a lot of fun, and we were winning—much more fun than losing for sure. He had been a bartender at the beach for years and decided to get a degree and now had his own business. He married a girl he had just started dating who turned up pregnant. They had two kids and had been married about fifteen years. I was super attracted to him, but he was drinking heavily by my standards, and I really didn't think we were a match, though I was having fun. He started talking about how he and his wife had partied so hard that it became an issue. She was home raising the kids but day drinking with his friends while he was out busting butt to make a living. The marriage ended. He went on to tell me that he had dated someone for a while, and she was the love of his life but had passed away. His eyes filled with tears. I felt so bad for him. "Oh my goodness! I am SO sorry. What happened?!" He shook his head gently, fighting back tears. Then he told me that he would have to tell me later. Shortly after that turn of events, he said he had to go, so we went outside. As soon as we were alone, he asked me if I wanted to have sex. I laughed out loud. "I do appreciate your candor, but I'm going to have to decline." He was a great kisser. On the way home, his car was ahead of mine and at the stop sign he got out of his car and walked to me to tell me that I had a front light out. I told him thanks, but I thought he was going to ask me for another kiss. He chuckled and said, "Oh, yes, that too." Then we kissed one last time.

He texted me later to say what an awesome lady I am. I was definitely attracted to him, but that party boy lifestyle didn't jive with me. Of course, I was curious about how the love of his life had died. I assumed that if it were cancer or a car accident, he would have told me. I was thinking suicide or a drug overdose. Turns out that he may or may not have pushed her down on the ice, causing a life-ending head injury. Wow, no wonder he cried; that is tragic. Someone also told me that he had a live-in girlfriend when we went out. Months later I saw him at a bar and I quickly slipped out before he could see me. The following week he texted me saying that he had lost my number and wanted to go out again. I told him I met a great guy and that I fixed the car light. Both lies. It seems that fixing the light was as challenging as meeting a guy.

63. Grouchy

It was the end of 2020. COVID still had a firm grip on the country, cutting off the dating habits of the elderly and sequestering me with a bunch of surly teenagers. I was initially attracted to Grouchy because he seemed like a silly, fun guy from his photos. I came waltzing into the Old West–style wooden bar on December 27. He lit up when he saw me, which is always a welcome response. I went right up to him and hugged and kissed him before he could stand up. It took him by surprise. He later told me that he knew that I was the one, not "the ONE," just the person he wanted to date for a while, based on my confident gesture of affection.

I have often wondered if most women greet their dates with a handshake because men often seemed shocked by my easy greeting. I am very happy to be there and to meet someone I had been corresponding with. Grouchy had two young sons but only fifty percent of the time. He had sent photos of the gifts his sons had bought for him for Christmas. Win or lose, I wanted to meet him. He was drinking some kind of Irish beer. He was fun and engaging. His wife had cheated on him. (Oh no, I thought, because I KNOW that can be a challenge). He asked me how many guys I had dated, and at the time it was thirty-nine. He emphatically told me that I would stop at forty, that HE would be my last guy. I liked his confidence. In fact, I liked him. He wanted to take me out for New Year's Eve. I was excited; Grouchy seemed like a keeper. He had me checked out to see if I was a security threat. I rather liked that, it seemed so "the spy who loved me." Can't remember the movie but it seemed sexy to me, don't ask why. We went for a walk in the park a few days later. In the light of day, it became clear that we had zero in common and in fact he really didn't understand any of my stories. He didn't laugh at the punch lines. We ran into one of my teenagers who had been jogging. It was a brief encounter, and I purposefully shuttled him away from her because other than once by accident, nobody had ever met one of my dates. At the end of that date, I decided he really wasn't the guy for me. I wasn't attracted to him in that way.

I had promised to go with him on New Year's, so I made good on that. He picked me up and had a sport coat on. He looked very handsome. We went to an Irish bar and although it wasn't the Four Seasons, it was fun and I had some drinks. We started talking about sex and I was intrigued. Turns out that Grouchy was amazing in bed. I decided that I might have a go at this. We dated for about five weeks before I realized that he was not a happy camper. He thought of himself as fun-loving and silly but he liked to argue for no reason at all. He was a know-it-all and argumentative. It wasn't a great combination. His favorite line was, "And your point is?" I strive for a harmonious relationship. As I tell my teenagers who seem to have the opposite of that goal, I want to live in peace and harmony. I certainly don't want to agree on everything, but I don't want to fight 24/7 either. He would argue about songs and who sang them. He would argue about car registration policies. He actually told his sons not to grow into a shoe size over 13 because they would have to custom-order shoes. I said I think Amazon has shoes over size 13? Grouchy insisted that Amazon doesn't carry size 13+ shoes! The final straw was when I had been to the grocery store then we had dinner with his mom and went to a bar afterwards. I was especially irritated by the arguing. I hugged him and said, "I can't come in, I have groceries in the car and I'm tired." He didn't hug me back and said smugly, "Okay, fine, be that way," then stormed into his house. Was he a four-year-old? After that, I hadn't seen nor heard from him for a while, maybe three weeks.

I started to wonder, as I often do, did I act too fast? We went out again. It went well and we had fun. He asked what I wanted to do in terms of the relationship. I said let's take it one day at a time. We continued to talk and text. Turns out his ex-wife was a factor in his outlook on relationships and hindered his ability to move on. He wanted to take her back to court because she was shacking up with a guy. Mind you, she probably made $25,000, while he made about $300k a year. He insisted that he didn't have another choice, since the divorce agreement says if she cohabitates, her alimony ceases. His young son asked why he was taking their money away and the caring dad told his child, "I am not taking YOUR money away; I am taking some of your mom's money because she broke the agreement." I pointed out that her money IS the child's money, and it will affect his standard of living when he is with his mom. Nobody listens to me especially when they are obsessed with their ex. The opposite of love is not hate, it's indifference. Hate leaves you connected to your ex. We went out on Valentine's Day, and he met all my teenagers, their friends, and boyfriends. He made them laugh so that was a plus. I bought him his favorite beer, then I stuck kiss emoji stickers all over the box. He asked, "What is this"? I said, "Excuse me?" He asked where I found his brand of beer. Still befuddled and a little pissed off, I said, "Did you mean to say thank you?" At dinner he proclaimed that Valentine's Day is just a made-up holiday by Hallmark. We texted the next day and then I never heard from him again, which is probably for the best. Is it me? Could you have stayed with him? I tried. I really did.

Fast forward two years later, somehow we reconnected. Truth be told, I saw his profile on Facebook dating, so I decided to give him a like. He messaged me and then I texted him. God as my witness I was NOT going to ask him out, but I did tell him that he was the longest relationship I had. By long, I mean two months—sad I know. My friend said I should ask him out, but I stood firm. It took him several weeks, but he eventually asked me out. We went out and to my surprise, Grouchy was much happier. We had fun. He bought a Jeep and did Jeep things with people. He acquired two puppies, and he loved telling stories about them. He let go of his anger towards his ex-wife. We ended up going out three times; each date was a lot of fun, but each date was only a few hours. Maybe that was the reason we were having so much fun? We ended up not going out again. I have thought about asking him out again, or texting him *what's up?* but I haven't. I know it's not the happy ending that people crave, especially my aunts, mother, kids, dog, friends, and hair stylist. I am comforted knowing that he was able to move through his difficult divorce and in the end, chose happiness with his Jeep and dogs.

64. Lax Player

In my part of the country, lacrosse is life. Kind of like football in Texas. Kids grow up playing lacrosse before they can walk. Lacrosse has paid for a lot of kids' college educations. I tried to get my kids into lacrosse, but it never stuck for any of them. Lax Player, as you may imagine, played lacrosse in high school and college. These guys tend to have womanizing reputations. He went to an exclusive private high school, and his friends had lots of money. It's interesting how people want to bring up money and social status upon first meeting someone. I find it rather boring.

Lax Player had been married twice. The first one was when he was young, like so many others. He divorced the second one because his wife basically hated him. Like many other wives her age, she didn't want to have sex, but also stopped hugging, touching, or kissing him. The last straw for him was that after being away on a business trip for several weeks, she didn't pick him up from the airport (which he could have let go of because she was the one taking care of the kids while he was away). When Lax Player walked through the door, she wouldn't even glance up from her phone to greet him. This was the defining moment in their relationship. Still, he really wanted to work it out because of the kids. He suggested that they go to counseling. She declined. She basically said, "Nah, I'm good, we should just get divorced." Wow. Lax Player was super nice, and I had a good time hearing his stories, but there was zero chemistry. He didn't seem fun at all. I could have been wrong. I assume that he felt the same way because I never heard from him again. Until . . . about five years later I messaged him because his young son-in-law passed away. We made plans to go out several times but it never happened. Oh well. Perhaps, once a lax player, always a lax player.

65. Feels Like Home

When I got married, my husband told me that under no cir-
cumstances would I be permitted to boss him around or tell
him what to do, wear, buy, etc. I stuck to this even when he
decided to wear khaki pants and a khaki shirt or some other ill-fated combination of clothes. When my close friend of
thirty years would see a man with stripes and plaid, she would
say, "His wife hates him." This is hilarious and sadly true, but
in my case, I had to look the other way. My mother-in-law
had bossed her husband up one side and down the other. She
was a lovely woman, but the nagging was relentless, and it
was painful to witness at times. I was super vigilant with my
ex because I wanted to honor his wishes, and he was younger
than me. A lot younger, so I didn't want to get into the habit
of telling him what to do. I didn't want to be his mom. I secretly hope his second wife bosses him around relentlessly. It
seems like most wives are bossy. It's what they heard growing
up. It's all they know. It feels like home on both sides. My
friend gave me some great advice. She said, "Honestly, I think
you are too nice. Guys need a challenge and like to fix things.
Try being mean." One night before bed, her live-in boyfriend
of four years said, "Goodnight, my love." She put her book
down and responded. "What did you just say?!" He repeated

it meekly: "Goodnight, my love?" "That's all you have to say to me? Why don't you call your colleague because apparently you have plenty of time to talk to her and not me." She pointed emphatically to the door. "Get out and go sleep on the couch." He looked at her bewildered. She then screamed: "I'm serious, GET OUT!" still pointing at the door. He took his pillow and sheepishly left. Next day: boom! Flowers arrive at her workplace. Next, her boyfriend drove an hour out of his way to take her to lunch. She is my idol. Maybe deep down, men want to be told what to do. Maybe they want to be yelled at. They do like a challenge. It is what they know. It feels like home.

66. Dates of My Past

I can't help but reminisce about some of the dates of my past.
I may have mentioned that I dated extensively prior to getting
married at age thirty-four. It is all a blur now, but I went on
many blind dates and in some ways, online dating is like that
because even though you see a photo and it's not truly as blind
as it was in the nineties, it is still blind. You have never actually seen the person. I remember being stunned on some blind
dates, wondering for the first hour why the hell my friend
would think I would like this guy. Trying to be nice and cour-
teous all while thinking, "Wow, my friend must not like me."
Still, I was always game for a blind date. There was something
mysterious and exciting about it. It was also flattering because
either your friends thought enough of you to set you up with
their favorite cousin, person, or neighbor, or they wanted you
to be as miserably married as they were. Whatever the case,
I was gung-ho. Out of the 150 guys I dated pre-marriage,
probably only five were blind.

I worked for the military, so there was a constant supply
of dates. It was a lot of fun. I recommend working with and
surrounding yourself with guys. Let's face it: they have their
flaws, but they are a lot more fun to work with than ladies. I

DO love my lady colleague friends, though, they have turned out to be some of my best friends!

A few noteworthy dates from that time: I went to the Philippines for an internship, and it was my first experience dating real men and not college kids. There everyone had so much disposable income, and I was wined and dined like a princess. Dating in Italy was fun too because in the land of love, PDA was the norm, and every restaurant was romantic. One of my favorite boyfriends took me on a hike, and somehow he got a splinter in his foot that I had to extract just as the sun was setting. It sounds gross, but it was romantic. You know how they say with the right person anything can be fun! Another of my favorite boyfriends of all time took me on our first date to Medieval Times, which I would dread going to now, but when you're young, everything is new and exciting. That was memorable because I ended up loving him. I once went out with a young guy, way younger than I ever had before. Our first date was wonderful because he researched and planned the whole date. We went to dinner and then on a boat. I was so impressed with this. With him being so young I didn't expect him to take charge, and it was rather nice. We ended up ditching the boat because it was quite crowded and instead kissed on a grassy knoll. I guess the difference between then and now, aside from my obvious baggage and age, is that then I was full of hope. With each one came a promise of hope. I wondered if this would be the guy I would marry and have kids with. I wondered where we would live. I had hope that we would stay married forever. Fast forward thirty years, and first dates have changed. These days, I am thinking, hmmm, can I spend more than two hours with this guy and still enjoy his company? I doubt I will ever get married, but I would like to find a person to get to know and stay with for a while. I guess you could say that I still have hope, just with a different goal in mind. That is why I keep trying because I know people do find their person, and I hope that it will also happen to me.

67. No Game

I met No Game in the parking lot because it was seven p.m. on a random Monday night in January. It was dark out and he was the only other person in the parking lot, so I just assumed it had to be him. He seemed rather cute and nerdy, which is a plus. He was a nice guy.

We walked in and were seated at a table in the corner. He had been married twice with only one child aged seventeen. He was astounded at my number of kids. Sometimes I think guys start doing quick math on the cost of so many kids. They can just multiply what they have spent by four. The date probably ends for them right there. On the other hand, I think moms do the quick math on how hard it is to raise one teenager, let alone four, by yourself, with no time off.

No Game had been on a cruise to Italy, Dubai, and Greece, by himself. This impressed me. Most people I met had never been overseas, and going alone was kind of a bold move. Although it was a cruise, so that's not nearly as brave as going to a foreign country and winging it. No Game worked for a family-owned business. He talked a lot and didn't ask any questions, which is typical. Overall, it was a good night, but there was no real spark or connection. He did say he'd like to see me again. I probably would have gone out with him again, but I never heard from him. Maybe he expected me to text him, but I didn't. No Game was nice enough, but there was no attraction, laughter, or reason for me to want to see him again. He had no game.

68. Tonsillectomy

Did you have a tonsillectomy when you were a kid? They were so common back in the day. It seems like everyone had one. I had one when I was thirty and no, unfortunately the guy I called Tonsillectomy wasn't an ENT. He was one of the fewer than 5 percent of the guys I dated who had never been married and never had kids. I shouldn't really be fascinated by such a creature because did I mention that my own very attractive brother is also a member of this club? It's a club envied by all married men, secretly or outwardly. It's not that my brother didn't want to get married or have kids, it just never worked out for him, yet.

It didn't work out for Tonsillectomy either. He was seven years younger than me, but according to him, he had always dated older women. He had gone to the same school as my kid, not at the same time, LOL. We both loved the school. We had planned to meet at a restaurant that was closed, due to COVID, so we walked around instead. It was late, old person late, about eight p.m., and nothing was open. We walked and talked. He was tall and stocky, bald and Middle Eastern.

What I can tell you is that he kissed by opening his mouth and sticking his tongue down my throat. Like we were twelve. My first thought was, now I know why he's not married. Honestly, it was horrendous. Turns out that some of my friends actually like this tonsillectomy style of kissing—who knew? Our second date was a trip to Costco. Ironically, my slogan from the very beginning of my dating endeavors was to "Make Costco fun again." Meaning I wanted to meet a guy where the simple things were fun again. Was this a sign? Maybe I had willed it. It was Costco after all, but unfortunately, it wasn't fun. He didn't speak to me at all. There was no joking, no feeding each other samples, no silly banter. I think he even shushed me at one point. Costco was a flop. He did not make Costco fun again.

69. Ethically Non-monogamous (ENM)

You will encounter a variety of lifestyle situations listed in peoples' profiles, especially on the free apps. Married people looking for a third person to have fun with. Married people looking to date. Bisexual guys asking if you are down with that. Some guys even state that they aren't interested in a transgender person. The one that gives me pause and a chuckle is the ethically non-monogamous or ENM (I admit that I had to look it up). It makes me wonder if the wife knows. I find it hard to believe that there are tons of guys out there who have wives (age fifty-ish) who have given them the green light, issued a kitchen pass, released the ball and chain, so that they can go mess around with other women. Maybe they think their wives know that they are dating but it has never been discussed? The approval has not been granted. I know that many women don't want to have sex anymore, but I don't think they are giving the go ahead for their husbands to get involved with other women.

Some potential pitfalls to this seemingly harmonious plan: What if she gets pregnant? What if he gets a disease? What if friends or family see him out with another woman?

What if he falls in love? What if the other woman steals from the bank account? What about the marital property?

Is your wife okay with the fact that your money—her money, marital money—is being spent on someone else? In relationships, there is a progression, and I believe most women and some men want to take it to the next level. They want to move from drinks and dinner to sleep overs to weekends away and so forth. What about that person getting into your head? When you are with your spouse are you thinking about the other person your wife has agreed to let you date? Your wife is OK with that? I think not.

70. College Friend

A college friend was going through his second divorce. He is adored by everyone. Even his two ex-wives still appreciate him. He is like a party in a bottle, and being around him is always a pleasure. He is also an honest guy and in touch with his emotions—kind of surprising because that doesn't exactly match up with his manly-man personality. He didn't cheat on his wives, which is remarkable. I had not seen or spoken to him at all in over thirty years. I made a joke on Facebook saying that if I could meet a man like my beloved sorority BFF who passed away from cancer in 2019, I would marry him. College Friend said something funny like "set the date." Then I said, "Is this a proposal?" So, we met for dinner. He was as charming and fun as he ever was in his twenties. He was just getting into the world of online dating. He dated a lot of women. Here is what I learned from him. Women are bold. Maybe you know this already. Women will FaceTime naked. They have no problem sending nudes. They are broken because most of them have been cheated on. Some seem to just want to hook up but eventually want more. They are confusing. He dated one woman for about six months. She had never been married and didn't have kids. She was a career woman with her own house. She was kind of funny about sex. She would sleep with him and do everything else but wouldn't go all the way. He spent Christmas with her, and he spent over $1,000 on gifts. He's very generous. It was right around that time that she started criticizing him. She said he needed to eat a burger because he was too skinny. That he shouldn't wear his shirt untucked. That she didn't like his ball caps. It was not going to work out.

He enjoyed dating around but had wanted to settle down, and he eventually met a Southern belle and fell hard for her. They dated for about five months, and then he had to move for a new job. He was going to ask her to move in with him, but she ended up sleeping with an old boyfriend. He was devastated. Eventually he took her back, but they broke up again. He recently got engaged to a lovely woman. I wish them the best because I adore him.

71. What? Why Not?

My sister chose this one for me. He was good-looking but not too good-looking, and his profile seemed appealing. He also had a lot of kids, which should have me running for the hills, but he was someone who could relate to my situation. He and I had gone to the same college. He played football. I sort of remembered him, but he didn't remember me because I was not a hot girl so was not on his radar. He was an attorney, and his wife of many years was mean to the point of abusive. He had to get out. His grown kids even supported his departure. According to him, they actually wanted him to leave. Of course, I only heard his side of the story. (I would really like to talk to some of these ex-wives, though.)

He was very interesting and insightful. As our date progressed, I was not sure if he was into me. Usually, I can tell. They touch you, there's a way they look at you, they sit close to you or ask questions. Some guys like you because you listen to all their stories intently and sympathize or laugh accordingly. I have experienced a range: from pure infatuation and lust to guys who took a phone call while I was sitting right there (see Towels Guy).

So, I was listening intently but half wondering, does this guy like me and do I like him? The jury was out. He got up and then came over and kissed me. Wow, he was a great, sensual kisser. After dinner was over, he walked me to the car, and we kissed three more magical times! At that point, I knew I wanted to see him again. Definitely. He texted me later that night. A friend once told me to stop texting thank you after the dates. She said to let them text first. They need to be challenged. So, he texted something sweet like, "I had a great time, I'd like to see you again soon." I responded with something kind but not too desperate. Then I never. Heard. From. Him. Again. What? Why not? This will remain a mystery. I will never know, and I probably don't want to. Don't ask questions you don't want to know the answer to. One of my all-time favorite lines. This is the one first date that truly got away.

72. Girls have changed.

I am part of a generation who grew up in the sixties. The women who raised us grew up in the forties and fifties. You know the drill: They were raised to be homemakers, to be submissive, to have children, and to be demure. A perfect summary of this is the high school home economics textbook passage from 1954 that basically explains how to make the home environment appealing for your hard-working husband. Things like having dinner ready, putting a bow in your hair, cleaning up the house, minimizing noise, never complaining, listening well, and so on. Honestly, this kind of personality gymnastics is probably what kept marriages together back in the day. One person catered to the other and made their life easier. But everyone can use that kind of support, no matter their gender. I don't have to tell you that women are a lot more confident, independent, equal in all areas, and adventurous today. My college friend who dated extensively told me tales about women who initiated wild sex in his truck on the first date. The interesting thing is while the promiscuous girls were fun, he had no interest in dating them long-term. Women may have evolved, but guys still don't like the idea of a woman having sex with multiple guys. Sure, they will partake in some hot, exciting sex, but they won't commit to that person. I think it is in their DNA, just like having sex somehow makes women become emotionally attached to their partners, guys want to know that they are the only one. My cousin had her own version of this story. She is twenty years younger than I am, so a different generation altogether. In the mid 2000s, at age 22, she had sex on the first date. The guy, roughly her age, said that it was a shame that she was so easy, because now they couldn't go on to have a relationship. She scoffed and said, "Ha! don't flatter yourself, bud, I have no interest in a relationship with you nor marrying you!" (another laugh) She told him that she got exactly what she wanted and asked for nothing more. Wow, you go, girl! She has been happily married now for ten years to a guy who she knew she wanted to marry on the first date. I am not sure if they waited or not; I will have to ask her. The point is that things have changed.

73. Baldy

He was fifty-three, good-looking, and bald. He was the only guy I dated who was bald. I never thought about that until I was reviewing the stats. Ironically, I like bald guys—I like all guys. My ex was bald, and I don't like him but not because he is bald. Maybe I was subconsciously avoiding that look? I met Baldy at one of my favorite places on the water. It was a very hot day, and I had to park a golf cart ride away from the destination. When I arrived, Baldy was at the bar. He was probably five ten, not the 6' he had claimed to be. His bald head was sweating profusely, but he was cute anyway. Two ladies my age were kind of listening to our first date unfold. Because we were once again sitting at the bar I could see them glancing at us and then whispering. Baldy had downed several drinks before I arrived. No big deal, lots of people are nervous, so I really didn't think anything of it. He was a divorced father of two boys who were roughly my kids' ages. He was in the finance field and worked from home. We were having fun, so we left and went to another favorite place and sat at the bar. It was nine p.m. at that point and I was starving. As I've said before I like when men take the initiative and order food. It's hot.

Baldy was not that guy. I don't like to drink and not eat; it's just not a winning combination. I ended up ordering food, and I still made him pay the bill. He drove me to my car, and we kissed under the summer moon. He was a good kisser, and we made plans to get together the following week. He started being text affectionate. He would text things like "I miss u," and "I really like you." I guess it was within reason though. Although he claimed to have left the stress of the corporate world, he never really seemed to be working. He moved a state away to get away from his ex after the divorce; however, he had two young sons. Turns out they never stayed with him, always with their mom. He did go to their games and saw them. I was starting to have second thoughts about seeing him again.

The night before our second date, he left me a voice message. It sounded urgent and he asked me to call him because he wanted to run something by me about his son. He was upset. When I called, I immediately asked him, "Hi there, is everything okay with your son?" He acted like he didn't know what I was talking about. I mentioned the voicemail, but still, it didn't ring a bell. He started talking about our date and was thinking about a picnic. At one point I told him that my childhood friend was just days away from dying, and he responded by asking if I liked cheese and crackers. I know men aren't the best listeners, but that response was completely off base. Then it hit me: Baldy was drunk. I had to let him go. Between moving a state away and not seeing his sons and now drinking heavily at home, I realized that we were not a match. That night he texted to ask if my kids were going to wonder why I was so tan. Um, not sure what he meant because the date was supposed to be at night. I let him go the next day, using my excuse that I am so busy with the kids because it was true, and I didn't want to hurt his feelings. I can't date a drinker. It's just not for me.

74. Gentleman

This guy was a class act. He wore a suit and brought flowers. It was such a sweet gesture, and no other guy had done that except Yankee Fan, but he had already known and loved me. Gentleman was twelve years my senior and it showed. Once men are beyond age sixty-two, they start to show their age. He had a photo of his younger self on his dating profile, and he was so handsome back in the day. Immediately after we sat down, he started telling me how he hated people who voted for Trump twice—a popular sentiment. I'm not one of those people who voted for him, but I love and adore several friends and family members who did. Gentleman was a carpenter and did work for his ex for free, which is kind. He had very interesting stories about working for wealthy people in the city. The most interesting part of the date was that through a DNA test, he discovered that he was adopted. He reunited with his biological family twenty years ago only to determine that he hated them and never spoke to them again. He was also furious at his adoptive family for never telling him, so he ceased speaking to them as well. I must admit, they did seem rather odd. Gentleman said when he walked me to my car that he thought he was probably too old for me. He told me to reach out if I wanted to see him again. As you might have guessed, I didn't. I thanked him for my flowers and the date and was on my way.

75. The Brother

Sometimes guys admire you from afar when either you are married, or they are married. Sometimes you have no idea who likes you until you get divorced and then they come out of the woodwork. This only happened to me twice. My neighbor's brother had been one of them. I was flattered. He was going through a divorce, slowly. In fact, I think they are still together, although he is living in another state. One weekend, The Brother came to visit me. We had been trying to connect for years, but with COVID and schedules, it never worked out. Finally, the weekend arrived. Luckily my mom was in town, so she stayed with the kids even though I slept at home every night.

The Brother stayed in a hotel, and I rented a car from Turo, so that my mom could use my car if needed. I was the designated driver, so I couldn't really drink at all. This was fine with me; however, I hate to drive, and the car smelled like smoke. It was killing me. The Brother was a Southern gentleman, and we had a fabulous time together. We went to a music festival on a double date with my sister and her hubs, and went to Fort McHenry. He was tall and handsome and funny, and I really liked him. He texted me to come visit him in his hotel, but I couldn't. Not sure why. My sister wasn't sure either. My sister's silence said it all. I told her that I know "I have had sex with less." As in *known* less, *liked* less, less *worthy*, less *fun*, and so on. The saying kind of stuck. Maybe I feared a real commitment? It could have been feelings for my Dream Man? In my defense, Brother was still married, though separated and not living with his wife. I'm sure he would be my man if he were divorced and lived closer, but such is life. Still, it was a fun time, and my sister was halfway ready to date him. Just kidding, though they both love football and she, like me, loves tall, big southern men.

76. An Original Thought

Reading profiles gets old. My married friends loved to do it for fun. After a while, you really get tired of hearing this stale and overused profile line: "If you don't look like your profile picture, you have to buy me drinks until you do." Guys, newsflash number one: girls are not going to post a bad photo of themselves. It's your fault for picturing a fifty-something as a thirty-year-old in a size zero body. Profile photos can't show tone, mood, attitude, or excitement. Newsflash number two: Do you think you are the only guy that has thought of that? Do you realize that about 30% of all profiles have some version of this?

The worst was this guy. He started with "I would like to add," but he hadn't said anything prior to this harsh statement: *"If we meet and your not the person I liked in the pics u posted and talked to. No deceiver will be tolerated. I will turn and walk around and be on my way. That means you can't be trusted. Ever! I am truthful and try to keep things up to date. Be the same."*

I would guess that he's not getting a lot of interest with that intro. My point is that guys complain about this when you ask how online dating is going for them. I started to realize that it is them and not the women in most cases. There are not tons of girls posting photos of when they were thirty years old or forty pounds lighter. Guys, wake up and keep your fantasies in check! I once told my sister that in some ways, guys are an older version of their eighteen-year-old selves and they are wondering while I am in mid-sentence how I perform in bed and what I am willing to do. Guys, I implore you to have an original thought. You are not the first one who posted that line about looking like our photos, and it makes you look more shallow than you already are.

77. Hiding Something?

A Sunday date in September on a dockside bar. I arrived first, which rarely happens. Most guys get there before me or show up at the same time. I was starting to worry that I was getting stood up. He finally arrived, and I was honestly relieved. We hugged and kissed hello. There was an immediate spark and a connection. He was very short and young-looking and had a positive disposition. He had never been married—a twelve-year and fourteen-year relationship. I called him a drink bully because he was trying to make me drink tequila. He felt bad later. We kissed in the parking lot. We went on two more dates. One was amazing and romantic at the top of the Four Seasons hotel. He asked me when the last time I had sex was. It had been a few days: Dream Man strikes again.

Turns out that he hadn't had sex in a few years, so he said. He was a scholar and a gentleman but also lots of fun! At one point I marveled at how young he looked and jokingly asked for his license. He wouldn't give it to me, and I didn't think anything of it until a few days later. Then it hit me: His phone was unlisted too. It bothered me but I continued to see him sporadically. I assumed he was married, although it didn't seem like it. In May, I invited him to join my friend and me on a rare trip to an upscale hotel restaurant in the city.

He met us there and we had a lot of fun. We ended up at my house and thankfully my kids were asleep. He and my friend were really drunk and loud.

After that episode, I had not seen Hiding Something in six months. I was avoiding going on his boat for a variety of reasons. Mainly I didn't fully trust him not to kill me. Thanks to those *Dateline* episodes. We were meeting somewhere, then we were suddenly heading to his boat. This time I obliged. What the hell. Might as well, right? It was a magical day. It was close to eighty degrees in November. The boat was really nice. We drank champagne, got silly, and had sex. Before you judge me, it was our sixth date, one of those days when I didn't have a care in the world. It was all about me. I had a fabulous time and made it home safely by six p.m. My Dream Man wanted to see me that night too, but I gracefully declined. I just couldn't. Hiding Something and I continued to text over the years. We would go out occasionally. To the Four Seasons lounge and once restaurant-hopping in Annapolis. Six months later, we met my "best advice ever" friend and her husband for drinks one night. Since that night I have not seen him and it has been years now. We still text and I would love to see him again, but if I don't that is fine too. He is definitely hiding something.

78. Doc

Doc showed up in a blazer and khakis. He was shorter than I had imagined but very attractive and stocky, which is nice. He was fun and animated. He used to be a doctor, but his license had lapsed. Hm, is this something that happens? It didn't seem like a common scenario. Not quite a red flag, but I assume things weren't going well for Doc. We met at a romantic restaurant that I had never been to before and sat on opposite sides of a cozy booth. He was funny but kind of odd. He was talking a mile a minute, and it was hard to keep up with his stories. He was very intense. At one point, he came over and sat on my side of the booth, which was fine, but it wasn't as comfortable as it had been with some of the other guys I've dated.

Some of his stories weren't suitable for a first date. For instance, he talked about how his brother was his dad's favorite, and this clearly bothered him his whole life. Doc went on to explain that when his dad was on his deathbed, his dad took Doc's face in his hands (he took my face in his hands to imitate the act) and then his dad uttered these dying words (as doc held my face an inch from his), "Son, you were always my favorite." I giggled nervously and pulled away. Meanwhile, Doc shed a tear. The reenactment was too much for him, I guess. I was thinking WTF is happening here? It was then that I realized that Doc had issues. I've dated many guys with daddy issues. We are from a generation of dads who were meant to work, not emote. That said, Doc took it to another level. Within thirty minutes of meeting him, he was crying about his dad who had passed away several years prior. Doc was very animated the rest of the night. It was a bit of a roller coaster but better than sitting at home. He walked me to the car, talking nonstop, and then suddenly asked me what was wrong. I have no idea why. Maybe my face showed that I was on the Doc roller coaster. We kissed several times. Despite his erratic behavior, I might have gone out with him again. Not because I'm a glutton for punishment but because I wanted to see if it was just first date jitters. Maybe he would have been calmer on the second date. I also wondered about his medical license. I'm sure there's a story behind that as well. He texted afterward but he never asked me out again, and I have to assume that I probably dodged a bullet there.

79. Friends with Benefits

I met a guy for coffee, not my favorite kind of date because I don't drink coffee. It is bright, so they can see my flaws, and there are many at this age. Coffee shops are full of hyped up people who can hear your awkward first-date conversations. Friends with Benefits was attractive and quiet in a sultry way. He was confident. Normally when a guy is married and just looking to hook up, he saves you the time and effort of meeting up by just stating it in his profile, or at least asking during the messaging phase. Most people are up front because it's easier to put it all out there via messaging or text. They don't want to ask in person, and then get a drink or hot coffee thrown in their face. Friends With Benefits didn't pre-brief me on his intentions, which would have saved both of us a trip to the coffee shop.

His story is the same one we've heard time and again. FWB was married for twenty-two years and had grown kids. The thrill was gone. No shit, Sherlock. Do you think the other marrieds are out there getting butterflies every time they see their spouse of twenty, thirty, or forty years? I'm not saying the love must die, but the *thrill* is gone over time. I didn't tell him this because I had just met him, and it was Christmastime after all. He was still married because people like being married. He said it was "just for the insurance." I guess people stay together for the money also. FWB just wanted to hook up now and then. He said we could do other things besides sex. Thanks, FWB, appreciate the offer. But I was not interested in such an arrangement. I told him that I knew some people who might want to partake in such an arrangement. I shopped him around, but there were no takers. In fact, they laughed. He was actually very attractive, but I guess most people have affairs organically. Finding them on a dating app might be less romantic, and they'd never be able to say that it just happened. There are all kinds of people on dating apps. Some are looking for a threesome or to hook up when passing through town. Recently an exceedingly attractive guy asked if I would date him knowing he was bisexual. No shade at all, but I politely declined.

80. Freak Show

Old-school guys want to talk on the phone. Maybe that's a good thing, because you might be able to eliminate a guy with a high-pitched voice. Be honest, ladies, it's not a turn on, am I right? My guy friend once met a girl who had significant trouble speaking English, and he didn't realize that until they met in person. I usually prefer not to talk before a date, but to each their own.

I talked to this guy on the phone for about an hour. He had been divorced for fifteen years and had been on 500 dates. This is not an exaggeration: over 500 dates. I'm sure I gasped when he told me, but he swiftly explained that I was on the same trajectory. Yikes! I shuddered at the thought. Could that be me? Is that where I was headed? The crazy thing about the 500 dates was not the 500. It was that he had only been on two second dates—only *two* out of 500!!! How is that possible? He said it was because women lie. About what? He said weight, age, details of their lives, and so on. "Wait a minute," I said, "you mean to say that over 498 women lied on the first date?" I'm a confident person, and I certainly don't lie, but after we hung up, I realized that I can't beat those odds. I realized that he was obviously still in love with his ex-wife. I get that, I really do. At first, I admit I compared guys to my ex. I came to realize that I would never be able to replace him, especially since nobody else is the father of my kids.

Freak Show described his ex-wife as "sooo beautiful." Mrs. Freak Show had left him because, according to him, she was a party girl and unfaithful. She thought he was boring. She went on to marry a wealthy guy, which I'm guessing was a huge ego blow. Tragically, the former Mrs. Freak Show and her wealthy party boy husband died in a boating accident. Freak Show was not a suspect in their deaths, in case you were wondering. It was a late-night drunken mishap, and they weren't wearing life jackets. Freak Show asked me out, but of course I canceled on him. I mean, really, what was the point? I sent a text asking if he truly wanted to meet someone or if he was still pining over his late wife. Don't ask me why I did this, because normally I wouldn't say anything. Okay, okay, that's not true. But it needed to be said, don't you agree?

A few months later, he texted me on a holiday, and lo and behold, I agreed to meet up for coffee. I wasn't going to, but he insisted on driving to my town, so I figured why not? I have to say that this was the most bizarre experience of all my dates, pre- and post-marriage. So, we're talking hundreds of dates. He started firing questions at me, an interrogation of sorts. Then he started doing the math on some of my responses. He questioned my age, which is current on dating apps but somehow, he thought I said fifty-four and I was fifty-five. Then he started asking me how long I had been married. I normally said eighteen years, but it was seventeen years and five months when he left and nineteen years one month when the divorce was final. Plus, we had met about nine months prior to getting married, so eighteen seemed about right.

He didn't come right out and call me a liar, but it went something like this: "So, if you were fifty-two when he left and you said that you were married at age thirty-four, it doesn't add up." Newsflash: I was not lying. I had no reason to lie. Nobody cares about exact dates; they just want to know if it was a month ago or a few years. In my case, I only want to know if it's been less than a year, because I am going to assume the guy is in a ho phase. He started saying, "Wait, how can that be right because you said you were divorced four years ago, but if you were thirty-four when you got married . . ." It was unreal. I realized he was just there to catch me in a lie. I'm so glad I wasn't excited about this guy and so glad I didn't drive an hour to be called a liar. Obviously, he was scared of relationships and chose to focus on catching women in lies rather than trying to date. I wish you the best in your pursuit to find liars. Buh-bye, Freak Show.

81. So Nice

Some guys are just so nice. This one was divorced amicably with no kids. Much easier to walk away when there's nothing to keep you connected. We met for dinner. Within the first second, I knew I could never kiss the guy. He was wearing a crossing guard vest, and that kind of ruined it for me. I'm not a clothes snob. I'm not one of those women who dates guys based on their choice of watch or cost of their suit. Sorry, I can't tell the difference. It's not what impresses me. With that in mind, I decided to give him a chance. He had been an electrical engineer since age sixteen. He worked in the city and lived an hour away. Sometimes while on the date, I started feeling as if I dated this version of the same guy a few years ago. He was very similar to many other guys in that he talked about himself the entire time. He did tell some very interesting stories. His dad died in a car accident, and his stepdad was murdered. He was also fairly well traveled, so he talked about places he had been. It was not a bad date per se, there was just zero attraction on my end. We really didn't have anything in common. At the end of the night, as predicted, he mentioned having had a great time getting to know me. Uh, I never said more than two words. He asked me to go out again and I smiled and said sure, that would be nice. What was I supposed to say? He was so nice, after all. He's the only guy who kept texting me for years to check in and ask me out. I told him I had met someone, and that was true. The last text he sent went unread. Sorry, So Nice, I wish you the best.

82. High School

Well, well, well . . . a football star from my high school days reached out to me via one of the dating apps. I can't see so well without my granny glasses, and I didn't realize it was him at first. I guess the fact that he used to have big hair and was now bald had something to do with it. It had been nearly forty years since high school, but I still had the giddy schoolgirl feeling while getting ready for our date. He picked me up because I knew he wasn't dangerous. I had seen him at our reunion a few years prior. He was very attractive, and we had a good time. He still held some kind of football record, which I found rather attractive. Although he has tattoo sleeves and possibly other tattoos that I couldn't see, he preferred his women to be tattoo-less. I was surprised by this. He had been married once and had a young daughter. He had other long-term relationships. He was a successful guy and seemed really great. Probably the most impressive thing about him was that several of his friends had made bad life choices, and things didn't turn out so well for most of them. He too was predetermined to meet with a similar fate, yet something within him led him to a path to success. Once you reach your fifties, you see how the story ends for the people who were once full of hope and promise. Many people who set out on a path of opportunity found that their choices led them to rehab, disaster, loss of families, and even death. In his case, it was the opposite, and there was comfort in that. I'm not sure why we didn't go on a second date. Perhaps because I was focused on another guy who I had just been out with. Later I ran into High School at a local diner. The wait for brunch on a Sunday is always long. I was with my mom, and he was with a buddy. We ended up chatting with them for a long time. My mom was drawn to his buddy. She suggested that I go out with him. I had to break it to her that the buddy was married. Sometimes moms know best, and sometimes they don't notice the ring. It was really fun catching up with him. I'm so happy that his life turned out so well. He will meet someone because he is great-looking, successful, and tall (which is really the only thing that matters).

83. Recovered from Everything

We texted for a while because the kids had an away tournament, so it delayed our meeting. He was intrigued because we lived within a few miles of one another but had never met. I really loved his voice, and he made me laugh. When we finally met up, I saw him pull into the parking lot. I hopped out and made an attempt at being funny. We hugged and I kissed him on the cheek. He asked if we could do that again. He was adorable and always wore a ball cap. Guys have a really hard time coming to grips with hair loss, so it seems. When the waitress came, I ordered a drink that they didn't have, so I opted for a Diet Coke instead. He ordered coffee, Coke, and water. It was then that he told me he is a recovered addict and can't ever drink. In fact, later he told me that if I ever saw him with a beer or a drink, it would soon lead to his ultimate death. This was ideal for me because I didn't want to drink, but sometimes did to make the other person feel okay. His stories were very interesting. His first wife passed away at a young age. Then he remarried and had two stepdaughters. From the minute we saw each other, the chemistry was undeniable. He was so open, so vulnerable. He actually teared up on the first date. I can't remember why, but his life story was heavy.

Afterward we talked in the parking lot. Then the un-
thinkable happened: He started to smoke. He asked me if it
was okay, and I said sure, which was a lie. I am highly sensi-
tive and probably allergic to smoke. It makes me physically ill
to be around. I decided to ignore the smoking. We went out
several more times, and one day he surprised me with roses.
I was giddy. He was an amazing man, and I have never met
anyone like him. His life's mission is to help others stay sober. He dedicates a lot of time to this. I once joked that I was
number five on his priority list, and he said, "No, you're actually number eleven, but you came up fast from twenty-one."

I'm no stranger to addiction. My dad died of cirrhosis at
age fifty-two; it really wasn't the skateboard for the elderly. I
struggled with alcohol in my teens and twenties but am in a
good place now. I can go out and have a drink or none, which
I usually prefer. He laughs at my drinking stories from my
past because they are so minor compared to what he has en-
dured and heard from the true addicts. One story he told me
I'll never forget. He had been sober for eight years, and something triggered him. He got in the car and started driving to
the liquor store. All the while he was crying and screaming
at himself not to go, tears running down his face. An inward
and outward battle against himself. Still, he went to the liquor store, bought his drink of choice, and guzzled away his
hard-earned eight years of sobriety back into the dark world
of addiction. This was twelve years before I met him.

Recovered from Everything knew his way around the
bedroom. The sex was amazing. I felt like an amateur compared to him. Having sex with him was like a carnival ride.
We dated for a few months. During the time, I wasn't sure

about being number eleven, and I really, really, really hated his smoking, even though he never smoked around me. Out of the blue, he canceled a date and then we faded out. I am not going to beg someone to date me or see me, so I let him go. We kept in touch, and I missed him and the crazy sex. Three months later, he told me that he stopped contacting me because he wanted to hook up with a girl he had been seeing for a while, on and (mostly) off. He told me that I am amazing, he has feelings for me, he loved being with me, I was incredible. He knew I was looking for a committed relationship. He told me he has no idea why he hooked up with her because he didn't like her nearly as much as he liked me. He ended up doing it anyway. Just like the trip to the liquor store. I have gone out with him a few times over the past few years. The chemistry was still there. I will love him always and forever; he is an amazing man. I had to walk away. Every now and then I still call him for advice. I hope that never changes.

84. A Break

I hadn't been on a date in over four months. After Recovered from Everything, I really needed a break. I'm not going to lie, it kind of bothered me because I really liked him and saw potential in our relationship. I was lying low, trying to regroup, and wondering what I should do differently. I was contemplating throwing in the towel altogether. I was not on any apps, that is for sure, and I wasn't planning on ever going back. To those who say, "watch, she will meet someone when she least expects it", or the ever-popular one: "Stop trying so hard and it will happen!"

Okay, grandmas, thanks for the optimism, but that is not how it works at this age. If I just sit at home, walk my German Shepherd, go to Target, an occasional happy hour, a nice, single fifty-year-old will not fall into my lap. I hate to disappoint but it's just not gonna happen. This is useful advice for someone who is twenty years old, maybe thirty, but not in the fifties dating game. It reminds me of the line in the 2014 movie *The Other Woman* that Leslie Mann hilariously delivers: "The last time I was single, the dating pool was everyone. Now it's like a shallow puddle of age-appropriate men who are old and gross!" I was taking lots of time to catch up on sleep, going out with my mom, to ladies' nights out, and enjoying dinners with my cousins. After four months of this, I became restless and decided to just look on Match for free. After a few weeks, I broke down and paid but only because it was half off. I talked to a few guys. Nothing exciting, but that old familiar feeling of being at a middle school dance when nobody asked me to dance came flooding back. Messaging and even giving a phone number to a guy and then not hearing from him. It was affecting my ego and my desire to date. I decided to be pickier this time around. Maybe that was the issue? I mention this because it happens to the best of us. Sometimes you need a break, or you don't. Either way, you do you. Eventually my drought ended.

85. Dr. Dolittle

This guy was persistent. He started texting me a lot. He mainly sent photos of himself with a squirrel on his shoulder, with a turtle, with his giant dogs, with a bird. You get the idea. Dr. Dolittle was almost begging me to go out with him. I really didn't want to. I let him go unread for a few days because my heart just wasn't in it. Then he suggested that I bring my sister along. I had already brought a friend on a date, so it seemed only fair that my sister should suffer through a first date as well. So, I obliged, and we met at my sister's favorite Italian restaurant. My BIL wanted to tag along, but we drew the line there. Having my BIL there would have been intimidating.

I was late. I never wanted to be a minute late because at our age we don't have much time. Not really, the truth is that guys were often early, so I never wanted to keep anyone waiting. It's rude and selfish and gives a bad first impression. I had my sister drop me off so she could park. I knew he was already inside because we had been texting. He was shorter than I thought he would be, but not bad-looking. We hugged and sat down. It was August. Probably ninety-five degrees. I soon realized that our favorite place didn't have air conditioning. The sweet owner insisted that the A/C was working. Maybe they didn't want to turn away customers, so they lied.

It was hot as hell inside. We chatted until my sister arrived. I mentioned that he should have been a vet because of his obvious love for animals and he said, "Why would I be a vet when I am highly successful in the finance field?" *Oh, brother.* I hate men who brag. If you are wealthy, I will find out in due time. It really has no bearing on me unless you wish to pay for my hundred kids to get a college education. But congrats, Dr. Dolittle, I am happy for you and your insecurities that prompted you to tell me that. My sister came in without her glasses. She only had her sunglasses with her. In the excitement of her first date, she left them in the car. I never noticed, but she said later that she could not see anything. That made me laugh. He talked about his kids, parenting. He declared that if the parents are good, the kids will turn out well. Sorry, I beg to differ, but I let that go. He ordered a double martini while my sister and I drank Diet Cokes. He talked about the school my niece was going to in the fall. His kids had also gone there, and turns out his neighbors' kids went to Harvard and Yale from that public high school.

He talked about his ex-wife. Same old story: she acted old, never wanted to do anything, no spark, and she didn't love his giant dogs the way he did. He talked a lot about his dogs and used their names. He was really into animals in case you didn't pick up on the context clues. At one point, one of my kids texted that she needed a ride. A family had taken her to an event, and I thought they were bringing her home, but she needed a ride. "Oh my gosh!" I said. "My kid just texted and needs a ride." Well, Dr. Dolittle thought I had texted my sister to suggest ditching him. I would never do that, except that one time when the guy was trashed. Even in a 100-degree restaurant with a guy I'm not attracted to and will never see again. I explained the situation, but he was convinced I was lying. I went to the restroom because it was a twenty-minute drive to get my kid. It was then that one of our favorite couples walked in. My sister couldn't see and didn't realize it was them until they said her name. She was understandably flustered because since I was absent—it appeared that she was on a date! LOL. Soon I sprang out of the restroom, saw the four of them making small talk and burst into laughter. Then I hugged our friends before warning them about the heat index in the restaurant. They had already been introduced to Dr. Dolittle and I giggled again at the thought of my innocent sister being caught on a date. When we were in the car, I asked her if she would date Dr. Dolittle and she nearly screamed an emphatic NO! Actually, she may have said, "No way in hell," and she is not a cusser. I laughed. I never heard from Dr. Dolittle again. It was sweet of him to take us out, and my sister enjoyed hearing about the new school. That made it worthwhile.

86. Too Skinny

I've dated a variety of guys, but I don't have a type because I find that so boring. When you get married, you have a type, but until then mix it up. He showed up to the date and I almost gasped. He was the size of a skinny teenager. In his defense, he did list his weight in his profile. It's hard to estimate how weight will look on a person. He said he was 150 pounds and six feet tall, but I swear he looked like 130. By anyone's standards, he looked malnourished. I prefer dating someone taller and bigger than me. I'm not a small person, and being with a small man makes me feel bigger. Yes, it is fucked up, but it is what it is.

I have dated guys who are shorter than I am and smaller than I am, so this is not a complete deal breaker. Some guys, whether short or tall, just exude spunk, personality, charisma, and confidence, and that is attractive. Other guys suffer from what my brother calls "Short man's disease." You know the type, when a guy must compensate for his size with a sports car, or possibly a jet. The jet would probably make up for the size honestly. Just kidding.

Too Skinny was from New York originally. He had traveled for his job, leaving his wife to take care of the kids. One day, he came home from a trip to a completely empty house.

She had moved out of the house without saying a word. He was dumbfounded and distraught beyond words. He rushed over to his neighbors to share the agony. Turns out the neighbor had helped her pack because his wife was having an affair with the neighbor. He punched the good neighbor right in the face. We went out twice. He was nice, but there was no connection and I could just not get past his size. Sadly, Too Skinny had cancer when he was young, and I fear that it may have returned because he could not eat. Both times we were together he ordered food, had one bite, and then said he just couldn't eat anymore. I really hope he's okay.

87. Too Nice

Do nice guys finish last? Can a guy be too nice? This is a question that you have to ask yourself at some point. If I made a graph of all the guys I dated, how many of the nice guys would I have been attracted to on the first date? Possibly zero.

I guess a graph is not needed to illustrate that. I went on a date with a very nice guy, maybe Too Nice. He was polished, respectful, interesting, polite, and fun to be around. He had been in the military for thirty years. Since I had worked for the military, we had been to many of the same places. His wife cheated on him for years; however, he wasn't officially divorced. I think that alone makes him a nice guy because for the sake of their son, he was hoping things would work out. When I met him, he had not dated for four years but was branching out into the world of dating. They had just sold their marital home, which was a breakthrough. There was an upward momentum, two dates, talking on the phone for hours, and then it suddenly changed. He cancelled on me twice in one week. It gave me pause. Was it just logistics or was something up? I suspected the latter because when you're first dating and you like someone, you really want to see them as much as possible.

He said many things that made me think he really liked me, but one I'll never forget. He said that kissing me was like the Disney castle fireworks. Wow, that was so sweet! It made me feel great about myself. After canceling two dates, the momentum had changed for me, maybe not for him. You'd have to ask him. Then I started to replay our long conversations to look for clues. He had told his wife he was going to start dating. She even suggested specific apps that he should try. She'd had a boyfriend for the past four years and seemed to really embrace his plan to date and hopefully meet someone. One night, she started drinking and decided to look at the phone bill. She noticed that he was chatting with women. She confronted him and said she wanted him back and that they could work it out. He said he had no interest in getting back together with her, but I have to wonder. He was a nice guy with solid core values, integrity, and high standards for his behavior. I liked him, but those Disney kisses were awkward, and I didn't know how to change that. Still, I wasn't going to let him go. Nice guys may finish last but honestly there aren't a lot of them out there who remain single. I wanted to hold onto him while I figured out if our awkward kissing could turn into more. I wanted to figure out if he was still in love with his wife and would end up trying to work it out again. I agreed to meet him at his house. Yet another decision I would come to regret.

88. Crazy STBExW

Too Nice was definitely nice; there was no question about that. Normally by the fifth date (or sooner) guys expect sex. They have waited patiently, spent their hard-earned money and time in pursuit of the prize, and by the fifth date, the time has come to get it on. We set up a fifth date at his place. I knew nothing physical was going to happen because you can't really go from awkward kissing to full-on sex without adding alcohol—a lot of alcohol. Maybe it's just me, but that friend zone started to creep in, and we were kind of at the point of no return. Initially I texted some excuse to back out on him, but for whatever reason, I ended up moving forward with the plan to meet at his apartment. I knew better, but I'm always caught between following my intuition and questioning whether my intuition is just an excuse to protect my heart. In other words, is my intuition a cover for my underlying fear of commitment? No matter, in this case, I ignored my intuition and went to Too Nice's apartment. I sent my sister his name, address, phone, photos, and workplace. He met me outside and showed me where to park. Meanwhile, I was scanning the parking lot to see if his soon-to-be ex-wife (STBExW) was lurking in the bushes. Sure, she had a boyfriend, but she was having trouble getting used to the idea of Too Nice dating. Bitches be crazy; sometimes it's true.

It was a fairly nice place as apartments go, I guess. Typical bachelor vibes though, but whatever, I wasn't planning on moving in. We hugged and kissed briefly. Let me clarify: it was a friendship type of kiss. Our relationship could be classified as platonic other than him saying he was crazy about me or falling for me on one of our long phone calls when I couldn't be sure whether he had been drinking. I am pretty sure he was though.

Let me set the scene for you. We were sitting four feet apart on his theater-style chairs, fully clothed, talking and barely holding hands, just holding the tips of our fingers. Very odd. He never offered me water or anything. After two hours of talking, I suggested that we go get something to eat, but it was lost on him. The night before on the phone, he had talked about ordering food, but I guess he forgot. I was contemplating leaving, wondering why I was even there. All of a sudden, there was a banging on the door. Not a polite knock: almost like a police invasion. I was like, OMG, here we go. I knew immediately that it was his crazy soon to be ex wife. He was shocked and panicked.

"Oh my god, she has only been here once!" he said. Then I heard the voice of his young son: "Daddy?" Then the banging and yelling continued. She was not happy at all. I was horrified. I would have called 911 if that child had not been there. He asked me what I wanted to do. Considering the options, I decided to hide in the bathroom. I was thinking that they would come in for a few minutes and then leave. LOL. He let them in and STBExW is screaming at him that his son had called twenty-five times. He told her to calm down for the child's sake. The verbal fighting ensued. They were loud, then he whispered that I was there, still hiding like a coward in the bathroom. I would have been texting my sister, but I was intent on holding the unlockable door closed so she or the child wouldn't barge in. Then she started directing her anger at me, screaming, "Well, did you tell her we kissed the other night?" He calmly said, "Now, now, you know that isn't true." Meanwhile, I was rolling my eyes, wondering why I even bothered dating and as always blaming it on my ex in my mind. I had been happily married; I should not be dating!

Prior to this little altercation, I had already made my mind up that if STBExW so much as called me and hung up, I'd be finished with Nice Guy. She had threatened to because she had seen the cell phone bill with my number. Obviously, given this insane scenario, I was way more than done. He told STBExW: "Clearly, you've been drinking." The child said, "No she hasn't, Daddy!" How did I suddenly get in the middle of a Jerry Springer episode? Eventually, Too Nice came into the bathroom. I was in disbelief, with my hands over my face. I was kind of laughing, but it was more like crying in disbelief. I was in shock even though I knew damn well this was going to happen. He asked me what I wanted to do. I told him I would stay there until they left. Shaking his head like a scared little boy who has been caught being naughty, he said, "Oh, she's not leaving, no way!" Mind you, this guy is a six-five, former military man, and he was terrified of his cheating, crazy soon to be ex wife. He gave me the option to leave without meeting them. The apartment was the size of a postage stamp so there was no escaping without meeting them. Finally, I dusted myself off, fluffed my hair, checked for mascara under the eyes, and burst into the scene with my head held high. I managed a confident and friendly "Hi there!" No response. She was sitting with her arms crossed. The child was kind of giggling at the scene. I turned to leave, and she said something like, thanks for *drinking* my wine? What? No matter, he escorted me out the door, and I said bye-bye, looking at both of them and kind of waving. Incidentally she looked nothing like I had imagined. She was nearly fifteen years younger than me, and since he kept taking her back despite her having a boyfriend, I imagined her to be exceedingly attractive. She was not. I hurried down the hallway half-scared she would run out and yank my hair or worse. He offered to walk me to the car, apologizing profusely. I hugged him and said, "Take care," meaning I would never see nor talk to him again as long as I live. I got in my car and peeled wheels to get out of there. I immediately called my Ohio BFF, and then my Dream Man. My sister was asleep or she would have gotten a call too. I was shaken to the core and questioning my life's decisions. Too Nice and his crazy soon to be ex wife probably reunited. I wish them and the adorable child the best.

89. A Woman's Intuition

Much has been said about following your intuition. If something feels out of place or suspicious, it probably is. I went to a renowned perinatologist. Once he told me that the key to his success was not his intellectual prowess nor years of experience. He said it was because he followed the instincts of his female patients and listened to their concerns. He did this because he learned early in his career that there is something about a woman's intuition that is mostly spot on. A few dads have told me that they instill this in their daughters. Don't wait around to see what happens, go with your gut and flee the scene.

A few stories must be told to corroborate this, which is something that can be felt but not seen or heard, like faith. My ex was having an affair for at least nine months prior to his departure. The Visa bill never lies. He was acting out of character, like dropping the kids off at the beach then leaving the next morning at seven a.m. He usually never woke before noon on weekends. Never. He asked me if he should go to a coworker's mother's funeral. He rarely if ever asked me what to do. He bought the kids birthday gifts. I'm not sure he even knew when their birthdays were. I asked him if his girlfriend bought the gifts. Looking back now, I'm sure she did, but I was half-joking. The Italians have a saying: *scarsando se dici La verità*. It means "joking but actually serious." It applied here. Once he was condescending toward me. At that point, I just asked if he had a girlfriend because he had never treated me like that before. On another occasion, he took a long walk with the dog. Again, he'd never done that before. He ran into my nephew and brother-in-law. He made up some excuse about why he didn't see them or hear them yelling his name. Obviously, he was talking to his girlfriend or his divorce attorney. In retrospect, I do wonder if my ex was sleeping around other times during our marriage. Once, about five years into the marriage, he came home wearing a complete outfit from Abercrombie. Jeans, a shirt, and a long sleeve shirt. I was confused. He was not a shopper, yet he said that he went to the mall. The mall? I asked him if his girlfriend worked there. Other than photos we had taken of the kids with the Easter bunny, he had not voluntarily set foot in a mall since he was sixteen. He also started working out, which is a telltale sign of cheating. That was about ten years before he left. He claimed it was because of his migraines. I walk a fine line between intuition and wondering if maybe I'm not cut out for dating and relationships. In any case, trust your instincts, your intuition. Always.

90. It's me, not them

Recovered from Everything and then Too Nice, or rather his crazy soon to be ex wife, nearly ended my dating career, but about six months after the dust settled, I jumped back in again. Maybe I'm a glutton for punishment. Sometimes you just think it's not worth the hassle anymore. I have no regrets. My dating had slowed down. I used to date twenty guys in a year, and now it has been four guys. For the record, I never set out to be a cereal dater. I don't know if that's ever anyone's goal. I thought I'd date five, ten, maybe twenty guys at the most, then stay with one for three years or more. I always hoped the guy I was meeting up with would be the one or at least the one for now. It just wasn't in the cards for me. I watched other people get divorced and get remarried in less than a year. I decided to focus on other things. I obviously don't want a relationship, or I would have been with one of these guys. I guess I thought it would hit me like a ton of bricks then I would run off into the sunset. Maybe I'm too picky. I tried for a relationship sometimes even after we parted, but nothing lasted. I ponder why I couldn't make it work with any of the guys that I dated, and I think it was mostly my fault. The trouble is that I genuinely like everyone, and it's difficult for me to discern between those who are a match for me and those who are not. I wonder if I was too quick to dismiss some of the guys who may have been a good fit. I wonder if something was holding me back. Maybe my ex, not that I would ever take him back nor want to be in the same room as him, but was I trying to replace him? Maybe I worried too much about whether my suitors would mesh with my kids. Having so many kids makes it tough. Just the mere thought of bringing someone home to hang out makes me cringe. Someone was bound to protest. Someone would think I could do better. Someone would dislike the guy. Maybe Dream Man prevented me from seriously considering other guys. The fantasy of being with him may have blocked my ability to give others a chance. Maybe the fact that I only have three actual dating outfits was preventing me from getting past the third date? In any case, I don't blame any of the dates. Clearly, it's me not them.

91. Trend Worth Trying

I have noticed a trend: lots of people in their fifties reconnect with their first love from high school or college. You know back when you were young, hopeful and whatever the opposite of being jaded is. The couples who reconnect seem very happy. My theory is that the rekindling connects you to your youth and the way you felt when you were young—excited for the endless possibilities awaiting you back then, still believing in love and fidelity and that proverbial picket fence. Being exempt from a long "to do" list that involves twelve loads of laundry, fixing or cleaning something, or driving a kid somewhere, or worse, teaching someone to drive. You were once free to travel the world, hang-glide, bungee-jump, swim across the bay, be promiscuous, become a CEO, or have perfect kids who went on to find a cure for cancer. Many things on this list were still attainable when you were young. These rekindled romances re-open the door to all of those possibilities. It truly feels like the first time, as the song goes. Your brain involuntarily connects to your younger days just by being with that person again. It is romance muscle memory.

My cousin suffered through a thirty-year marriage. Her ex was always angry, always yelling at the kids, always criticizing everyone. He left her in the end and by doing so he did her a *huge* favor. She moved back home and started dating her high school sweetheart. Instant love. The high school sweetheart happens to be intelligent and loving, family-oriented, handsome, and wealthy. We should all be so lucky. Look around, it is common. There's also something mysterious and alluring about unrequited love. Perhaps the greatest love stories of all time are based on wondering what might have been. Ask around, check Facebook, or use Google, maybe your childhood love is single. It is definitely something to consider looking into.

92. Mental Health

This guy was smitten. He started showering me with compliments and accolades within the first five minutes, looking at me like he was in love. This was a red flag. Hearing you're beautiful, you're a great mom, you're all I can think about . . . these are things I'd been longing to hear. He also brought me gifts: Swedish Fish, flowers, and a candle. How did he know gifts are my love language? So maybe he wasn't polished and maybe he was a fifty-year-old groupie, following his favorite hard-rock band to see them live in concert, over twenty times. He was into me and let's face it, I prefer guys who are into me. One little itty bitty problem: he had been going to therapy once a week for twenty-five years. This is great, right? A man who isn't afraid of therapy. A man who's in touch with his emotions.

By the second innocent date, which was weeks after the first, because he travels for his job, I was starting to question some of his texts: I miss you, you're all I can think about, you are my dream girl. We had only spent four hours together. Still, I was in denial, thinking lots of guys know immediately that the girl is the one. At the end of the second date, I knew I had to put an end to the adoration and accolades. He explained that he had some serious mental health issues and had been hospitalized. I was scared that if we dated any longer, it could be a disaster. I ended things with him over text. He was angry, which scared me a bit. A few days later, the guy who never made it past a restaurant asked if he could see me one more time to perform oral sex on me. I laughed out loud, then called my sister. It was a bold request. How do I respond to that? Imagine going from a brief one-sided love affair to that, without massive amounts of alcohol. I did love the gifts and accolades which they call love bombing. Much like sweet kiddie cereals, you can't indulge in those at our age.

93. One Love

People are driven by the need to feel loved and wanted. Many feel validated when they are in relationships. My friend once said that people are meant to be part of a couple. We are happier that way. I could show her several examples of this being false, but I know what she meant, and for the most part, I agree. Wanting a best friend, a relationship, a lover is the reason I went on so many dates. Sometimes there can be a dark side to relationships. Relationship abuse is real. It knows no socioeconomic, age, or cultural boundaries. It ruins lives and permeates families. It is proactive to understand the signs of an unhealthy relationship. Having an awareness of these factors can prevent you from engaging in or initiating such behaviors. I would be remiss if I didn't mention a phenomenal organization that was born from the ashes of a 2005 tragedy at the University of Virginia. A beautiful lacrosse player who was days away from graduating, Yeardley Love, was beaten to death by her affluent ex-boyfriend while he was in a drunken rage. Her family decided to take action. Not against the ex-boyfriend, they had bigger fish to fry. They set out to educate youth about healthy versus unhealthy relationships, so they founded the One Love organization. They have online tools and webinars and are presenting the topic to high schools and colleges across the country. It is worth looking at their information. It is compelling. You may be surprised at the statistics. Perhaps you may recognize the traits of relationships from your past. If you have children, start educating them on the signs of healthy and unhealthy relationships, in an age-appropriate manner, of course.

94. Chance Meeting

I cannot remember randomly meeting someone at a bar, restaurant, event, or concert. Come to think of it, I did meet someone at a conference in Chicago when I was about twenty-nine. That was fun, but I only talked to him for about twenty minutes because he just wanted to hook up, and I didn't, so I'm not sure that counts. I never thought it was possible to spontaneously and unexpectedly meet someone. This is the main reason why I started the online cereal dating game. Well, I guess I was wrong. I admit it. I went to a small concert venue in my hometown to see Carbon Leaf. I was planning on going, then couldn't get a ticket; then I had one. It's all about who you know. My friend and her wonderful husband ran the entertainment, so they were busy taking tickets and working the event. I was kind of nervous about going alone, but I was happy to be there. A guy walked by, and I stopped him because I thought he was a friend of one of my friends. He wasn't. He was another guy who I had once seen when I was out with the Brother and wondered who he was. It is hard to keep people straight sometimes. Chance Meeting was very attractive and muscular, short, and Italian. He stayed by my side the whole night. My sister knew him from high school, and I was texting her about him from the bathroom. He had never been married and seemed like a very nice guy. It was all rather exciting. We chatted all night then we parted ways. I called my Ohio BFF from the car to tell her that she was right, a chance meeting actually happened to me. I think it helped that I was alone and approachable and not preoccupied with friends. I suggest trying that; do things alone. We did go on a date. He was very nice and respectful, a gentleman. We also met for happy hour once. It dawned on me a few months later that he had dated one of my Ohio BFF's friends. I sent her a photo and she had been out with him a few times. I'd like to tell you that we dated for months and fell in love and then lived happily ever after, but unfortunately that didn't happen.

95. Fun Fact

Ohio BFF, called to tell me that a study showed that married women are the unhappiest set of people in America. Interesting. Maybe you have heard this? Single women and married men are the happiest people. Based on a lot of married women I know, I might have to agree. I'd have to learn more about the study because if you don't work and you are married, you should be able to find joy with all that free time you have on your hands. If you are a working married mom, then I can see this being true. Think about the married women you know. They do it all with little time for themselves. They work, take care of and stress about the kids, take care of aging parents, do the housework and the driving, while the hubs is out playing golf. Whenever people say that divorce was the only way to find happiness, I think to myself we need to define happiness. There may be something to single women being the happiest though. I am very happily single, I am happy to report.

96. Blind Date

My kids cannot begin to understand the concept of blind dates. If someone set them up, they would immediately have that person's Snap, Insta, and TikTok accounts to see what the person looks like, hear their voice, study the side of their ear and everything else there is to know about that person. Like writing letters and drive-in movies, blind dates really are a thing of the past. If you've never been on one, you've missed out because it's an honor when someone thinks highly enough of you to set you up with someone they really like. Of course, this can be tricky because let's say you work with someone and she wants you to date her brother. She knows you will be a match because you have so much in common and he's such a nice guy! You agree to meet him, and well, let's just say he's not nearly as handsome, funny, or perfect as his sister thinks he is. She excitedly asks you how it went. Do you lie? No, you go out with him again, but the second date is worse. How do you explain to your fun coworker that you don't have even a smidge of attraction to her brother? She's going to be disappointed and possibly resent you for it. The better option is just to tell her that you're a lesbian, otherwise there will be a wedge between you forever. Girls hold grudges. I am speaking from experience.

Getting married was a relief knowing I wouldn't have to go on blind dates anymore. And now here we are, right back where we started. A close friend set me up on a blind date with her son's boss. Finally, someone offered to set me up and I was game! She showed me a photo of him while I was driving, so I had a general idea of his looks, but probably couldn't pick him out in a lineup if my life depended on it. He texted me. I reported this to my friend. She was perplexed and even asked, "Who?" She had forgotten all about the set-up. This was probably a good thing. Less pressure. The Blind Date and I talked briefly on the phone, then texted a time and place to meet. I was looking forward to meeting him. At the time, I was taking a break from online dating. I was also getting too attached to my Dream Man again, so I needed a diversion as I always did when I was feeling attached to him.

I texted Blind Date when I arrived. I mistakenly thought he was in the restaurant, but they seated me at an empty table. Was I being stood up, or was he watching to see how I looked before he went inside? Did I go to the wrong place? He showed up about five minutes later. Blind Date was nice looking and he was a very nice guy. He had been divorced for six years and had never been on a date. Not one. I'm not clear why he got divorced, but it seems like his wife wanted out. He had been to Italy many times, and since I used to live there, I enjoyed his stories. He lived a simple life with his sons. All in all, I had fun, but it wasn't a match. He probably could have been over time. Who knows. Incidentally, he has the same name as Dream Man. Not a big deal except that he texted me later and I responded with "Thanks, Patrick." Not a bad response if his name had been Patrick. He responded, "You mean John?" Whoopsie-daisy. In all my dates and the many guys I've texted, I've not called someone the wrong name. Not once. That I know of anyway. I didn't think I'd hear from him again, but to my surprise I guess calling him the wrong name worked because he asked me out again and who am I to say no to a nice guy? In the end it just wasn't a match. My friend is not mad at me but it may have bothered her a bit.

97. Heard it all?

After over four years on the dating circuit, I had pretty much heard it all from guys whom I had never met. The guy who called for the first time to have phone sex with himself. The guys who are never going to meet you but just get off on talking about sex. The guy who you are really connecting with via messaging and boom, he ghosts you. The guy who gets angry at you. The guy who practically proposes on the phone. There were many guys who I messaged and talked to who I never met in person. The holidays came crashing in as always and that time is always hard for me. I needed a distraction during the holidays and my office was closed, so I dipped into a dating app ever so slowly and carefully. *Hmmm . . . let's just see who is out there.* Boom, a guy starts messaging me. We messaged for over an hour, back and forth, and I was grinning all the while. He was fun and we had a lot in common. Crazy as it sounds in that short period of time, I went from its just never going to happen to a glimmer of hope. Like a cancer patient, the only thing keeping you going at times is that elusive hope. Next thing you know, it's noon, and I'm in the shower getting ready to meet Heard It All for a quick coffee at Dunkin. Not my ideal first date and it probably won't work out, but it might. In the shower, I start having second

thoughts but after all it's just coffee. I am about to leave, and
he sends a message to ask me a question. A question about my
anatomy?! What the hell, is this really necessary before a day-
time coffee date? It was a very specific and detailed question
about my girlie parts. I was confused. He had to explain it to
me several ways before I understood. WTF. What the literal
FUCK? I did not measure up to the specific anatomy he was
interested in. As he put it, "It is not a preference, I cannot get
aroused by someone who does not meet this specific require-
ment." I called an expert on the subject, my sorority sister
who happens to be a lesbian. She explained it in detail and
even she was shocked at his audacity. I think she called him
a Fucking Weirdo, that made me feel better. He gave me the
option to be just friends. I told him I have enough friends.
So there's two hours of my life I can never get back. Lots of
guys toss out the topic of sex because they want to gauge your
interest, prude meter, or libido level. They don't want a repeat
of their sexless marriage, and I can accept that. I went from
getting ready for a meetup at Dunkin to shaking my head in
disbelief. Just when you think you've heard it all, another reason to be rejected. Note to self: lower expectations.

98. CAPS Fan

I met a guy and we chatted via message system and then took it to text. I liked him because he was a CAPS fan. I mean full-blown with the license plate and everything. Our first date was at a very romantic and fun place. I really liked my date, who was originally from New York. He was very fun and engaging. A really great storyteller. Wow, I really liked him. We walked around after dinner and then went to a coffee shop. Same old background story: He was going through a divorce, three kids, one was school-aged. No spark in his marriage or rather, it was over for a long time. CAPs Fan didn't have a job, which for some reason didn't bother me. He also didn't ask me any questions, nor really listened to anything I had to say. Maybe I liked him because he bought me a CAPs shirt. Yes, I can be bought, it is obvious looking back now. I ignored the signs that for me, this wouldn't work. Distance, no job, a young kid, leaving a long-term marriage to find "happiness." That five dollar CAPs shirt was blinding me apparently. He asked me to a CAPs game, which was a few weeks from the first date. I excitedly accepted. Finally, a guy was speaking my love language: gifts and a CAPs game. We also made plans to go out the following weekend. I was really looking forward to it. The place was an hour away and

I took the wrong exit. When I finally arrived, I immediately saw him in a different light. Maybe he was mad that I was late? He was loud and irritating and not listening to me at all. It was like he was attracted to me but didn't want to listen to anything I had to say. At one point, he was talking about how his divorce was hard in the beginning but now everything was wonderful. He asked me a question with excited anticipation: "Aren't you glad you're divorced?" My answer was immediate. Should I have lied? No! I am not happy that my ex left me and the kids. Our lives are not better without him. We loved him. We miss him. I spared him the truth and simply said, "No, I am not happy to be divorced; however, I would never take my ex back and I don't want to ever see him again, let alone have sex with him, but I am not glad to be divorced." (Especially on this date with you). Yes, it's me, hi, I'm the problem, it's me. I should have left after dinner, but I agreed to go on the Ferris wheel at National Harbor. It looks so beautiful from the Woodrow Wilson bridge. It was probably twenty degrees outside, and we had to wait for a long time in the freezing cold. This was a very cute gesture and with the right person it would have been great. I found myself wishing it was Hiding Something whom I had just been out with the previous week. Finally, we went in the heated gondola, and CAPs Fan just wanted to make out. Meanwhile his snot was dripping into my mouth. I was grossed out. I could not wait to get off the ride. We parted ways and I ran to my car then texted that I couldn't go to the CAPs game because of ride conflicts, which was true. I never heard from him again and he deleted me from the dating app. I don't remember feeling like that before where I really liked a guy on the first date and did NOT like him on the second date AT ALL. Still, he was a nice guy, and I wish him the best in his pursuit of happiness. GO CAPs!

99. My Three Sons

I've said this before and I will say it again: I really like when we message briefly, and the guy asks me out straight away. My Three Sons was that guy. We met up at a local bar. By this point in my cereal dating career, I had already been on dates at every bar and restaurant within a ten mile radius. I hate to admit this, but I have been on as many as seven dates at some places. Spread out over five years, so the staff turned over several times, hopefully. I had been to this place with You Never Know, and we had a lot of fun there. My Three Sons had recently lost his wife to cancer. I found out later that she was diagnosed and passed away within a month. Very difficult for him and the sons. We had a great time, there was chemistry, we were fist-bumping about loving Chris Stapleton, and several other things. It was a great first date. He walked me to the car and said he wanted to see me again and asked what I was doing the next night, then he laughed before I could answer. It's awkward at the end. You feel like you're seventeen again. Do you just hug them, do you kiss them? I am never sure what to do. I can't concentrate on what they are saying because I am fixated on this. I went in for the kiss and he said, "Fuck, yes, I want to kiss you!" Then I started laughing and it made the kiss awkward but fun. He messaged me his mobile number later that night and said he really enjoyed meeting me. We texted the next day because it dawned on me that I had met his wife about twenty years ago. Then crickets. This was not my first experience with a good date ending in silence, but I did not see it coming. Maybe he wasn't sure if I liked him? Yes, I knew better, but several days later I decided to text him. I said something stupid about having a good weekend, and I hope to see you again soon. Ugh, why did I do that? Clearly, he was not interested in me. I know that if he were, he would have asked me out. Some people never learn. Some people is me. I ended up sitting next to him at Jiffy Lube about three years later and pretended not to recognize him. LOL. Childish yes but I couldn't think of anything to say.

100. Message for Days

Speaking of never learning lessons, I broke my other rule and ended up messaging a guy for days and weeks. Probably only five weeks, but for me that is a lot. We shared a love of hockey so that helped because our team was not doing well and that kept the messaging going. He asked me out, but I couldn't go, so I kind of counted that as a date. Lying to myself. Lo and behold, I did end up meeting the guy for dinner. Miracles do happen. He was cute. He talked a lot about the politics in our town. He was originally from Chicago. Again, not my best date but I would have gone out with him again. He had been divorced for a long time because of no spark. He had had a girlfriend he was crazy about because they had "lots of sex" and she suddenly left him to move to Florida. He seemed more broken-hearted about that than the failed marriage. We texted a bunch after the date and planned on getting together but it never happened. If you're reading this Blackhawks fan with a hockey playing daughter, please ask me out again, I will happily go. Based on my experience, if you wanted to ask me out, you would have already. Lesson learned, maybe or maybe not.

101. Quiet Guy

Sometimes you just need to give the Quiet Guy a chance. Just like the advice of one of my favorite memes: Don't go home with the life of the party. Go home with the guy who makes sure the life of the party gets home. Instead of focusing on spark and attraction, ask yourself: has it worked out with the guys who I'm normally attracted to? If the answer is no, then maybe give the Quiet Guy a chance.

Quiet Guy and I were going to meet at a movie. Probably the ideal date for him because you don't have to talk. He ended up having to work, so I went to the movie by myself. I highly recommend it! Then he sort of begged me to meet up with him, so I obliged. I met up with him on a Sunday. At that point, my kids didn't care what I was doing or even know if I was gone, so I had additional free time on my hands. Quiet Guy was attractive. He was an only child, which I think is rare for our generation. He talked a lot about high school and his childhood. The problem with Quiet Guy (and quiet guys in general) is that it is hard to get to know them. Luckily, I had no problem talking, so I carried the conversation. He laughed at some of my jokes, which I am a fan of. He said that we really connected and that he had fun. While it wasn't one of my best dates, I decided to go out with him again. As he walked me to the car, he mentioned that many businesses are going cash free. This makes sense to me because of taxes and there is less chance of a theft. He whispered that there is actually a deeper reason why. Then he proceeded to ask me if I noticed that the QR codes always have three sixes in the number? Oh no, Quiet Guy, you're not going to say what I think you're about to say. I said no, I hadn't noticed, and braced myself for the next words. He followed up by mansplaining that six is the sign of the devil, and that is what is behind the cash-free business models. Welp, no second date for you, Quiet Guy. Next!

102. It Gets Old

I have to admit that over time, it does get old. Messaging people, not getting responses, looking at profiles that you are hopeful about, and not matching. Then comes the date. You're not really looking forward to going but you know you must "play to win." Working from home, or in a small company, or in a female-dominated career like teaching, you're never going to randomly meet a man. You just aren't. Sorry, rom-com fans, that's just for the movies. Yes, I am contradicting myself, but chances are you'll never just run into someone and it's going to work out long-term. I went on another date. A place with a nice atmosphere and close to my house. I found myself straining to hear at times, but I could generally piece together what my date was saying. We had a friend in common, an ex-husband of a cousin. This was common ground, so we discussed our mutual acquaintance at the beginning of the date. It was a great ice-breaker. He had the same old story; he left his wife because they had become just roommates. If I only had a nickel every time I heard that. He was nice enough but kind of a nerd. I like nerds, but honestly, I was bored. The odd thing about him is that he told a lot of detailed sex stories, including dates he had been on with aggressive girls and various threesome stories. I guess this was new territory for the nerd. I'm sure if I got to know him, I would like him, but after the date, I was feeling neutral. I would have probably gone out with him if he had asked me, but he didn't. I really didn't care. No hard feelings, I wish him the best.

103. Ego Boost

Sometimes when you least expect it, a little ego boost comes sailing your way. I was visiting my Arizona BFF. She and her hilarious bestie, son, and adorable daughter-in-law took me out to a karaoke bar. That was the last thing I wanted to do, being jet-lagged and now in my late fifties, so not up for as much as I once was. My entourage was so much fun, though, singing and dancing. The daughter-in-law kept grabbing the microphone from us to belt out a song. It was hilarious. We were all having a fabulous time. Still, I would have been happy to leave at any time. Suddenly, I noticed a cute guy who seemed to know everyone at the bar. He was chatting with people and making the rounds. He had fake glasses, was tall, former military, in his forties, and funny. When he heard I was single, he shouted, "Why in the *hell* are *you* single?!" That was flattering, especially coming from him. I thought he would try to hook me up with his chubbier, much older sidekick, but he immediately started flirting with me, making me laugh. I loved every minute of it. Eventually he was touching me, in a G-rated way. Then we started kissing! My friends were dying! Definitely not characteristic of me at all. I wasn't drunk, although he may have been. Kissing a hot stranger in a bar? I hadn't done that since college. The best part was that he never asked me to go home with him. It was just fun for now, a brief moment of pure joy. Yes, I know—he probably has a girlfriend or wife waiting at home, but I'll store that little ego boost and use it as needed. Sometimes it's fun to be single.

104. Choosing Dating Apps

At the end of the day, I believe in love. I believe you can have the all-out head-over-heels, can't think straight, can't eat, giggly, sparkly, love. It may only last a few months or a year, but it's not just for the twenty-year-olds. I saw it with my mom's second marriage. She was in her fifties and met the love of her life. And my aunt met her second husband in her sixties. He was Prince Charming himself. He made her life so grand. Her best years were with him. She travels with a framed picture of him. I know that you can have a later in life, passionate, best friend kind of love. He is out there, and he does exist. I have many cousins and friends in enviable long term marriages too.

For the record, I think all apps are the same. I have been on Match, POF, Hinge, Tinder, Bumble, E Harmony, Facebook Dating and others I can't recall. When people label a college as a "party school," I argue that all colleges are party schools because a. your parents aren't there, and b. There are tons of kids waiting to have fun, and c. nobody has any real responsibilities. Dating apps are the same. The dating apps are riddled with people looking to hook up, while some want long-term relationships and others want something in between. All of the dating apps have plenty of fakes, scammers and even 12 year olds posing as a grown man. The same types of people are on all the apps. I agree that some of the paid apps may be more conducive to those looking for relationships. I recommend browsing and not paying until you're ready. In the beginning, I was ready to spend money I didn't have for the chance at love. Toward the end of my run, I needed the money for beauty treatments, because let's face it, I was getting old.

105. Jeep Guy

I've noticed that the new midlife crisis car is a Jeep. Congrats, makers of Jeeps. It is a lifestyle. The Jeep owners have rallies, beach meetups, various functions, off-roading, and holiday lights parades. I met Jeep Guy on Facebook Dating. We had one friend in common. I decided not to text the friend because after all, the chances of us going out for a second date were slim. After a few days of messaging with Jeep Guy out of the blue, our mutual friend texted me to put in a good word for my date, which was cute. She is a beautiful person and one of the lucky ones who married her high school sweetheart, and they are still madly in love. If I'm being honest, I did not have a good feeling about Jeep Guy. We met at a restaurant; he was cute. We ended up talking and laughing for three hours. We have similar retirement goals, and he seems like a great guy, like my friend said. I admire him because he waited until his youngest child was out of college before divorcing his wife. I always feel bad for the wife because I am her in these stories of heartbreak and broken dreams. His wife never worked and gets lifetime alimony, so that worked out well for her. I have never heard of that before. I mean, he's not thrilled about that, but he fulfills his obligation to the mother of his sons. He is a good dad by all accounts. He made me laugh. He was looking for a long-term relationship and would even be willing to marry again. We went on four dates. I enjoyed each one immensely. For some reason, it just fizzled out. I can't explain why. Maybe we ran out of things to talk about. Maybe he just wasn't that into me. He's great though, and one of the hardest working guys you will ever meet. Years later I found out that he is happily coupled up.

106. The Writer

This Writer was a match made in heaven. He was in the military, had another career, then retired and wrote full time. Our first date was dreamy. We seemed to connect, and his kisses were on point. The Writer had written a nonfiction book. Of course I ordered it. He was also working on a fiction one. He had a whiteboard to plot it out and traveled to places that his characters would find themselves in. The Writer played handball, whatever that is, but he was the national champion for his age group. I really liked him after the first date. He was smart and fun. The second date was in my neck of the woods. The Writer had come upon heavy traffic on the way to pick me up. Not a big deal, except there was only thirty minutes to grab a bite to eat. I excitedly got into the car. Immediate vibe shift from the first date. The Writer was upset and agitated. I took him to a local bar, and he was not impressed—not that he should have been. It was just a quick bite. He made some disparaging comments about the town. Things were going downhill. Then he started criticizing me or rather the fact that my house had not sold. Second date: D-minus. I was not sure I wanted to go out with him again. He was condescending and snobby. A week later, he asked me to see a comedy show, so I reluctantly obliged. Sometimes I think I do not give guys a fair chance. Maybe I eliminate them too quickly. We had fun, it was a B-plus date. Then I had to leave because the kids got locked out of the house. He was this side of angry. He nearly yelled at me for not giving the kids a key. Truth is, we never used keys. The realtors kept locking the doors, and then we couldn't get in. I was not upset because I really didn't want to go up to his place and take it to the next level. I guess he did, I mean, he is a guy after all. He started pouting when I said I had to go. Then he gave me a quick kiss goodbye and said I hope it works out. He left me in the city. Yes, I was in front of a nice hotel, but he left. I hit it off with the Uber driver on the way there, so he picked me up and we had a few laughs on the way home. The Writer texted me the next day wanting his sunglasses back. I left them in my mailbox. He texted an apology three days later and I appreciated that, but once again, he just wasn't my guy.

107. End of an Era

Finally, I came full circle. It was appropriate that I closed out my dating escapades with the one who started it all. I had not seen Yankee Fan in four years. Of course, he took me to a Yankees/Orioles game. He looked great and was as chivalrous as ever: letting me go into the elevator first, walking me to my car after the date. All the things I love. It was great to see him, and he seemed happy; however, he was not as enamored with me as he had been previously. I am not sure why. Maybe he was seeing someone. Maybe he was just not that into me, or dating in general. Maybe he couldn't focus on me because it was one of the worst Yankee seasons in decades. Even if it had been a love match, he was living overseas for another three years. Plus, his one true love aside from his sons will always and forever be the Yankees. We may have lost in love that night, but the Yankees won the game.

I'd like to give you the happy ending that you yearn for, but my happy ending may just be that I can date anyone I want, whenever I want. I choose the coveted multipack of mini cereal boxes that we used to get every year on vacations to the Outer Banks.

108. More Cereal

Whether you date around, date a ton of people, or get lucky and meet Mr. Right on the first try, you do you. Just know that it usually takes a while to find your favorite cereal, and if you've never tried Cranberry Almond Crunch or Dunkaroos, how do you know if you like it or not? Meeting people can expand your world. It can make your life interesting. Each guy I went out with taught me something. Even if that something was that I really like ahi tuna. Let's face it, as you age, your priorities change and the guy you fell in love with in your twenties may not appeal to you in the least. I used to love the beach. I would obsess about the next time I could go to the beach. I have so many great memories of being there with my kids, my mom, my siblings, and my girlfriends. This year I realized: wow, it was never about the beach, it was about being with my people and getting away from the stresses of life. I don't have to be the same person or date the same person I searched for in my twenties and thirties. My kids are grown. I'm trying to figure out how to pay for college. I'm losing loved ones. I am facing my own mortality. I want to be with someone who I can cherish, who I can count on and rely on, and who wants to have a lot of sex. Mostly I just want to laugh with one person. Enjoy the ride, because your dating years are over before you know it and the cereal box is on the shelf, but it's empty.

109.   Best Laid Plans

Does anyone's life go as planned? I often wonder about this. I would guess that people's lives rarely go as planned. If yours has, congratulations. Cheers to you if you recognize your good fortune. I used to think mine did. I was living the dream. I had it all, and more importantly I KNEW that I had it all. Kids, a loving husband, close family, friends, my health, financial security, a beautiful home, wonderful memories of a life well lived. My sorority BFF's life did not go as planned; still, told me she had done everything she set out to do, which included getting a master's degree, living in Germany, marrying, having two sons, and being surrounded by a loving family and great group of woman friends. Sorority BFF sadly died of cancer at age fifty-four. Her only regret about dying young was leaving her sons orphaned, who were both in their young twenties. She was known to say, "why not me" instead of "why me." Her theory was that everyone suffers tragedy and heartache in life and it is the way you respond to those pitfalls that defines you. I have to agree with her because she was always right, but I don't think heartbreak is equitable.

Back to the lesser important subject of dating. Not everyone can have the same success rate in the online dating game—if success is defined as a long-term relationship or marriage. Outlook and attitude are everything in dating. Still, some people have all the luck while others just don't. In the dating game, the catch is that you don't know whether you're going to be lucky or not. It's worth a shot or perhaps many, many shots just for the life experience alone. Dating random strangers will give you more to talk about at the water cooler, than the shows you binge watched and the other mundane topics of daily life. I challenge you to learn something, in general, about yourself or about life from each new person you meet. A friend of mine told her widowed friend that she wouldn't recommend online dating after what I had been through. I had to jump all over her because to the contrary I may not have met Mr. Right part deux, but I would not trade the experience of meeting so many incredible men and laughing along the way.

110. Free Fallin'

I highly recommend adding tandem skydiving to your bucket list. This involves being hooked to a dive master's body, in a baby carrier situation. Then he (and you in the front) jump out of a perfectly good plane. It is a thrill and a rush like no other. Your life is quite literally, more than it has ever been, in that dive master's hands. If you have trust issues, you should definitely jump out of a plane attached to a guy. It will make trusting someone with your heart much easier. I went sky diving on my thirtieth birthday. It was in DeLand, Florida, with one of my best friends, a dad of three. First, there was a short training session. It seemed like a lot to remember, especially since I was nervous with anticipation and suddenly remembered the horror stories of parachutes not opening and the like. At the end of the session, the instructor—a buff, rugged former Navy SEAL—told the group, "Emotions are high, fear is a given, and if you forget everything you have just learned about skydiving, remember one thing. Just ONE THING." He was pointing up to the sky emphatically as if we were headed into enemy lines. "Do **not** grab your dive master's arms!" He stopped and eyed all of us. Everyone was out and out terrified, looking back at him, and some were debating going home. "If you grab his hands . . ." There was a frightening pause. "He can't release the parachute, and you will both go crashing to the ground to your untimely death." Okay. Note to self: don't grab the guy's hands. The analogy is a bit dramatic but the same applies to online dating. Remember one thing and one thing only: DO NOT give anyone money for any reason. Dating may not be the same as the rush and excitement of jumping out of a plane, but it will be fun, and I promise you will land on your feet.

111. The Stats

The guys I actually met in person/ went on a date with.

Met on dating apps	98%
Met spontaneously	1%
Blind date	1%
I knew them previously	11%
Paid without question	98%
Never Been Married	8%
Divorced because "lost spark" = no sex	75%
Still married "separated"	18%
Wives Cheated	13%
Had Kids	86%
College degree or more	58%
Just wanted to hookup	26%
Blew me off/ Never heard from again	8%
I didn't want to see again	28%
Dated more than once	30%
Could have had a relationship	58%
Financial issues/ poor	3%
Bald	2%
Very Attractive	88%
Made me laugh	85%

Enjoyed the first date	99%
Didn't drink etc./ Recovered addicts	15%
Drank excessively	3%
Drove a Jeep	5%
Wives were alcoholics/ addicts	5%
Had cancer previously or currently	3%

What I have learned about fifty-something-year-old men:
- They are a lot of fun.
- Most are very funny.
- They are generous and chivalrous.
- If they wanted to be married, they would be.
- They are particularly messed up when their wives cheat.
- They lie about height if they are under six feet.
- They want to have sex with twenty-year-olds.
- Most leave marriages for someone else.
- They always leave marriages to have sex.
- They are hoping for a supermodel.
- They're kids in a candy store with dating apps.
- They still love the chase and a challenge.
- They are short (most are five nine and below).
- They will contact you if they want a second date.
- Some want a do-over from their first failed marriage
- Some will remind you of your dad.

Advice
- Don't give anyone money—EVER!
- Give people a chance—step out of your type.
- Display a variety of photos.
- Show the real you. Post at least one photo without filters or makeup.
- Don't take it too seriously—most are one date max.
- "Like" and message a lot of guys and see if you connect.

- Men like to lead; let them initiate.
- Confidence and attitude make a difference.
- Don't get caught up on one guy too soon.
- Know that you WILL be rejected.
- Meet within the week.
- Have a quick "pre-date."
- Prince charming is not out there, but a nice guy is.
- Steer away from exceedingly handsome or buff
- You will meet great people and learn from them
- You won't meet guys sitting in your house watching Netflix
- Hug your dates they need to be loved.
- Some guys are very nervous
- If the profile says looking for casual relationship, believe it
- Some are scared of being judged.

Advice for Guys

- Don't give anyone money—EVER!
- Women will not look like their photos (we know how to take flattering pictures)
- Don't dominate the conversation
- Keep your bragging to a minimum
- Ask questions and listen to the answers
- Go on a brief date, set an ending time, so you have an out
- You are not going to find a perfect woman
- Be up front in texts about your goals
- Enjoy the company and experience
- Please tip the waiters well and be nice
- Farrah Fawcett or Christie Brinkley do not exist
- We look better than your mom did at this age
- The majority of women up to 90% can't achieve orgasm solely through vaginal penetration. (Yes! they faked it.)

Actual profile lines
- I don't want to be dragged around as an errand boy
- Please be beautiful, fit, athletic, emotionally secure, confident, affluent, with a strong self-image, and no kids at home.
- Looking for a pet mom for my dog
- No stay-at-home moms. I am not footing the bill for you to be lazy.
- Please look great in a bikini.
- I want a nice church-going lady who is also wild.
- I am in great shape, wealthy, and handsome.
- Please look like your photos
- I'm not trying to date a cartoon puppy
- If you don't look like your photos, you can buy me drinks until you do
- I am tired of hearing "you're a great guy" line. Save it.
- I can walk without assistance.

Need some dating coaching or advice?
Follow me on instagram: **@audieamae**

About the Author

Audie A. Mae hails from a quaint Maryland town south of Baltimore. She went to college on the Eastern Shore then moved to Florida, Italy, California, and Virginia, while proudly working for the US military. She met the man of her dreams in 2000 and lovingly raised four children. After her happily ever after crashed and burned in 2018, she and her four children managed to survive on their own. All four are now thriving college students. Audie A. works in early childhood education. She enjoys long walks with her German shepherd and traveling to see her beloved friends. And of course, she's still in active pursuit of Mr. Right part two.

This is Audie A. Mae's debut memoir written to bring hope, a bit of advice, and a few laughs to aging single moms everywhere.

www.ingramcontent.com/pod-product-compliance
Lightning Source LLC
Chambersburg PA
CBHW061144120626
46546CB00005B/1916